Anti-Inflammatory Soups

175 Delicious and Nutritious Recipes to Heal Your Immune System and Fight Inflammation, Heart Disease, Arthritis, Psoriasis, Diabetes, and More!

Stephanie Bennett

TABLE OF CONTENTS

INTRODUCTION

Inflammation is your immune system's response to injury or unwanted microbes in your body. It is a natural process and vital part of your body's healing process. When inflammation becomes systemic and chronic, however, it becomes a problem, and measures need to be taken. This type of inflammation serves no purpose, and can cause a lot of harm to the body.

As a nutritionist, I have clients suffering from a wide spectrum of health issues, and inflammation is easily one of the most common issues. Some of these clients are in constant pain, often excruciating. Migraines are a regular occurrence, and they don't sleep too well either. Their energy reserves always seem depleted and even sleep doesn't help, even if they manage to get a few good hours in.

I always suggest these clients to get a blood test for C-reactive protein if they haven't got one already, and if you feel you suffer from any symptoms of inflammation, I suggest you go to a nearby lab and get this blood test done right away. Chances are that your C-reactive protein levels are higher than normal, and the best way to manage this is diet. Shouldn't be hard though, considering how delicious anti-inflammatory foods are! Even if you do not suffer from chronic and systemic inflammation, incorporating anti-inflammatory foods in your diet will be one of the best decisions you will make in your life. You will notice the difference when you start. Your energy levels will be much higher, your mood will be uplifted, and you will feel more alive, in general.

This book has a LOT of recipes, and not every recipe might work for you. For example, if you're allergic to dairy or gluten, the recipes containing those ingredients will cause more harm than good. However, substitutions are possible for all of these, so you will be fine following this book as long as you keep an eye on the ingredients and use a bit of creativity where you have to! Once you understand the fundamentals of the diet, you will be fully equipped to create your own recipes from scratch!

In this book, you will learn all about the ingredients that are alleviate inflammation, and those that aggravate it, so you can make an educated guess for what's the best recipe for you, and what's the worst, even if you're out eating at a restaurant.

CAUSES OF CHRONIC INFLAMMATION

Medical science is striving to pinpoint the causes of chronic inflammation, and according to the Autoimmunity Research Foundation, numerous possible causes have been identified. This knowledge has mainly been derived from observational studies in which researchers can find correlation, though correlation does not equate to causation. Which is to say that while causes are identified by the studies, there is no scientifically proven concrete link between causes and outcomes. This uncertainty is an integral part of epidemiological studies, but they can still provide some very useful information.

Suggested causes for widespread chronic inflammation include:

- Antibiotic overuse and misuse (including in the food supply and through prescribed medications)
- Dietary factors (processed foods, unbalanced essential fatty acids, and chemical additives, among others)
- Environmental factors (endocrine disrupters and pesticides, among others)
- Use of substances (medications) that suppress immune responses, such as anti-inflammatories, antibacterial agents, and corticosteroids

In addition, **Medical News Today** ***(MNT) notes other factors that may play a role in chronic inflammation, including:***

- Autoimmune diseases
- Obesity
- Poor sleep quality and sleep deprivation

CHRONIC INFLAMMATORY DISEASES

The research goes on but quite a few diseases have been linked to chronic inflammation. In this section, we will take a look at some of these.

AUTOINFLAMMATORY DISEASE

According to the National Institutes of Health's (NIH) National Institute of Arthritis and Musculoskeletal and Skin Diseases (NIAMS), autoinflammatory disease is a rather new class that is quite unlike autoimmune disease, although the names are rather similar and they share some features. Autoimmune diseases are caused by the immune system attacking healthy tissue, leading to chronic inflammation. The reason for this is not fully understood by science just yet.

Autoinflammatory diseases can cause intense, chronic inflammation that can lead to symptoms such as fever and joint swelling. A few common diseases in this category are:

- Behçet's disease
- Chronic Atypical Neutrophilic Dermatosis with Lipodystrophy and Elevated Temperature (CANDLE)
- Deficiency of the Interleuken-1 Receptor Agonist (DIRA)
- Familial Mediterranean Fever (FMF)
- Neonatal Onset Multisystem Inflammatory Disease (NOMID)
- Tumor Necrosis Factor Receptor-Associated Periodic Syndrome (TRAP)

AUTOIMMUNE DISEASE

NIAMS says that autoimmune diseases also have a chronic inflammatory component to them. When your body sees its own healthy tissue as an intruder, it attacks it. Inflammation is one of the key signs of autoimmune disease, although, depending on the disease, other symptoms might be exhibited too.

More than 80 autoimmune diseases have been identified at the time of writing this book, and some of the most common ones are listed below:

- Addison's disease
- Ankylosing spondylitis
- Celiac disease
- Crohn's disease
- Endometriosis
- Fibromyalgia
- Grave's disease
- Hashimoto's disease
- Interstitial cystitis
- Juvenile (type 1) diabetes
- Juvenile arthritis
- Lupus

- Lyme disease (chronic)
- Multiple sclerosis
- Psoriasis
- Rheumatoid arthritis
- Scleroderma
- Ulcerative colitis
- Vitiligo

CARDIOVASCULAR DISEASE

The American Heart Association notes that while it isn't currently established that inflammation causes cardiovascular disease (diseases of the heart and blood vessels), it is usually present, particularly in arteries of people suffering from this kind of a disease. Multiple factors are associated with heart disease, such as tobacco use, high blood pressure, and high levels of "bad" cholesterol called low-density lipoprotein (LDL), etc., so managing these is key to preventing and managing cardiovascular diseases.

TYPE 2 DIABETES AND OBESITY

An article in the May 2, 2005 issue of the Journal of Clinical Investigation studied the link between type 2 (adult onset) diabetes, inflammation, and stress, and found a close correlation between inflammation and type 2 diabetes, mostly triggered by obesity. This research suggests that obesity activates multiple chemical responses in the body that result in extensive inflammation, and this inflammation further causes metabolic disorders like type 2 diabetes.

MANAGING CHRONIC INFLAMMATION

With advances in medical science, we have quite a few options for managing chronic inflammation. Some of the most popular options today are as follows.

NSAIDS

Nonsteroidal anti-inflammatory drugs (NSAIDs) such as ibuprofen or naproxen sodium (Aleve) are often recommended by health experts for managing and treating inflammation. However, these can potentially cause side effects, especially when used in the long term.

CORTICOSTEROIDS

These synthetic steroids are administered both orally and externally, and are great at suppressing the body's immune response. However, these too can cause side effects in the long run.

HERBAL REMEDIES

Minor inflammation can be managed by simple herbal remedies containing anti-inflammatory ingredients like turmeric and ginger. Combining turmeric with black pepper, coconut oil, or quercetin increases its bioavailability, thus making it easier for the body to absorb it.

LIFESTYLE CHANGES

Simple lifestyle changes such as exercise, yoga, meditation, better sleep, losing weight, stress reduction techniques, etc. can go a long way in managing inflammation.

ANTI-INFLAMMATORY DIET

The anti-inflammatory diet is a fairly new concept, and research is still going on. However, a review in the December 2010 issue of Nutrition in Clinical Practice notes an anti-inflammatory eating pattern which balances the ratio of essential fatty acids (omega-3 to omega-6 fatty acids) and consists mainly of fresh fruits, vegetables, legumes, and whole grains while reducing saturated fats (such as fats from meat) and maximizing monounsaturated fats (such as olive oil), is much better at managing inflammation than a typical western diet.

ANTI-INFLAMMATORY EATING HABITS

You are what you eat. Eat good, look good, feel good. Eat trash, look like trash, feel like trash.

FIGHTING INFLAMMATION THROUGH DIET

The anti-inflammatory diet has a very simple concept. When you plan your meals, you maximize the ingredients that reduce inflammation, and minimize/eliminate the ingredients that aggravate inflammation. Though, this is easier said than done.

We live in a world where everything, even food, is available at the flick of your finger. We are surrounded by delicious processed food with chemical additives, preservatives, and unhealthy fats. When such good taste comes with such high convenience, it is easy to give in.

However, if you do manage to overcome your urges, and decide to eat healthy, I'll tell you what you need to look for. Head to a nearby farmers' market and pick out fresh anti-inflammatory ingredients. Some of the most potent anti-inflammatory ingredients are listed under the next heading.

ANTI-INFLAMMATORY INGREDIENTS

Not all ingredients are created equal when it comes to the anti-inflammatory diet. Some are simply better and more potent than the others. I am a woman of science, and medical research has revealed some of the best ingredients for managing inflammation. If you're serious about this diet, you will do well to have all these ingredients on hand at all times.

BELL PEPPERS

Bell peppers—particularly red bell peppers—are a great source of antioxidants and capsaicin, both of which are exceptional at fighting inflammation. Add them to recipes containing turmeric for an anti-inflammatory bomb. They also contain quercetin, which enhances your body's absorption of anti-inflammatory curcumin. Be careful using these if you're sensitive to nightshades though.

BROCCOLI

High in fiber and immunity-boosting antioxidants like vitamin C, broccoli is a potent inti-inflammatory ingredient.

KALE

This vegetable is loaded with fiber and antioxidants.

SPINACH

Loaded with antioxidants like vitamin C and K, spinach is great at fighting inflammation.

TOMATOES

As long as you're not sensitive to nightshades, tomato is amazing at fighting inflammation, thanks to the lycopene contained within.

BLUEBERRIES

Blueberries are rich in antioxidants, and augment your immune system while fighting inflammation. Oh, and they taste absolutely amazing!

SALMON AND OTHER FATTY FISH

A good balance of essential fatty acids (omega-3 and omega-6 fatty acids) is absolutely vital to combat inflammation. Omega-3 fatty acids are anti-inflammatory, while omega-6 fatty acids are pro-inflammatory. Functional medicine specialist Chris Kresser notes that the perfect ratio of omega-6 fatty acids to omega-3 fatty acids is 1:1 or 2:1. The problem with the typical western diet is that this ratio is really unbalanced. The omega-6 fatty acid is so high in the western diet that the ratio can be as bad as 25:1! To counter this, supplemental fish oil rich in omega-3 fatty acids can be taken, or better yet, a diet rich in salmon and other fatty fish can be taken. These fish taste absolutely amazing, and are great anti-inflammatory ingredients!

NUTS

Nuts rich in omega-3 fatty acids are best. Some of these are: walnuts, cashews, almonds, pecans, etc. These have a high calorie density, so eat in moderation if you're looking to lose weight.

CINNAMON

Cinnamon contains cinnamaldehyde, which, according to an article in the January 2008 issue of Food and Chemical Toxicology, is a great at fighting inflammation.

GARLIC

One of the most potent anti-inflammatory ingredients, garlic has been used in home remedies since ancient times. Modern science too has now confirmed that garlic enhances the immune system, and is one of the best anti-inflammatory ingredients out there.

GINGER

Ginger adds an amazing flavor to whichever dish it is added, and boasts potent anti-inflammatory properties to boot!

ROSEMARY

This fragrant and flavorful herb is a potent anti-inflammatory ingredient. It goes especially well in a non-vegetarian dish.

TURMERIC

Turmeric contains curcumin, which many studies have concluded is great at fighting inflammation.

EXTRA-VIRGIN OLIVE OIL

EVOO is loaded with healthy fats, and contains oleocanthal, which is a potent anti-inflammatory compound.

GREEN TEA

Green tea is loaded with antioxidants, enhances the immune system, and has anti-inflammatory properties.

INGREDIENTS TO WATCH OUT FOR

While a certain ingredient might reduce inflammation in one person, it might do the exact opposite for another. Below is the list of a few ingredients that are common allergens, and if a certain recipe in this book doesn't help with inflammation, try eliminating these ingredients first.

The anti-inflammatory diet for every person will be a little different, and you are the only person who can find what ingredients suit you best. Below is the list of ingredients to watch out for:

- Dairy Products: A lot of people are allergic to casein, whey, and lactose. All three are contained in milk, and if you're allergic to even one of these, substitute dairy for nondairy alternatives such as almond milk or hemp milk.
- Eggs: This is an allergen that is hard to substitute in most cases. If you're baking, eggs can be replaced by flax eggs. Flax eggs can be made by mixing 1 tbsp ground flaxseed with 2½ tablespoons water and allowing to rest for 5 minutes until thick. This substitutes one egg in baking recipes.
- Fish: If you're allergic to fish, try shellfish instead. If you're allergic to that too, try chicken instead. Try tofu in fish recipes for a vegan dish. Soy sauce is a great alternative to fish sauce.
- Gluten: Gluten is one of the most common allergens out there. This protein is found in wheat, barley, etc. Two of my favorite gluten free grains are millet and quinoa.
- Nightshades: If you're sensitive to these, you should avoid eating tomatoes, tomatillos, goji berries, eggplant, bell peppers, chile peppers, and potatoes. Two alternatives are onions are garlic, but nightshades can never truly be substituted.
- Peanuts: Peanut allergy is quite common. It is a legume so substitute it with a nut you like and are not allergic to.

- Soy: If you're allergic to soy, you will need to read labels of all food items you buy. Tofu can be substituted by chicken, while soy sauce can be replaced by a spice blend of your choice.
- Tree Nuts: Tree such as almonds, walnuts, pecans, cashews, Brazil nuts, macadamia nuts, etc. are allergens to some. Try peanuts or a different nut you're not allergic to instead.
- Wheat: Another common allergen, wheat is easily replaced by buckwheat or rice flour.

THE COMPLETE ANTI-INFLAMMATORY FOOD LIST

BEVERAGES

POTENTIAL PRO-INFLAMMATORY INGREDIENTS (AVOID/MINIMIZE)

Soft drinks, sweetened (with sugar or artificial sweetener) || Soda, regular || Soda, diet || Milk, dairy || Liquor, hard || Liqueurs || Juice, sweetened || Energy drinks || Beer || Artificially or sugar sweetened drinks

INGREDIENTS THAT REDUCE INFLAMMATION (EAT THESE)

Wine (limit 4 oz.) || Kombucha || Coffee || Chai (with nondairy milk and no sugar)

POTENT ANTI-INFLAMMATORY FOODS (EAT A LOT)

Water || Tea (Particularly Green Tea)

CONDIMENTS

POTENTIAL PRO-INFLAMMATORY INGREDIENTS (AVOID/MINIMIZE)

Vinaigrette (store-bought) || Teriyaki sauce (store-bought) || Salsa, with sugar || Salad dressing || Mayonnaise (store-bought) || Ketchup || Cocktail sauce || Barbecue sauce

INGREDIENTS THAT REDUCE INFLAMMATION (EAT THESE)

Worcestershire sauce || Wasabi || Vinegar, all kinds || Vinaigrette (homemade) || Tomato paste || Teriyaki sauce, sugar-free (homemade) || Tamari || Tahini || Soy sauce || Salsa, sugar-free || Mustard, ground || Mustard, Dijon || Miso || Mayonnaise (homemade) || Hot sauce, sugar-free || Horseradish, prepared, sugar-free || Fish sauce, sugar-free || Anchovy paste

DAIRY AND DAIRY ALTERNATIVES

POTENTIAL PRO-INFLAMMATORY INGREDIENTS (AVOID/MINIMIZE)

Whipped cream || Sour cream || Nondairy creamer || Kefir, cow's milk || Ice cream || Heavy (whipping) cream || Half-and-half || Goat's milk || Cow's milk (all types) || Cheese, dairy (all types)

INGREDIENTS THAT REDUCE INFLAMMATION (EAT THESE)

Yogurt, Greek || Yogurt, dairy || Yogurt, coconut, plain, unsweetened || Yogurt, almond, plain, unsweetened || Soymilk, unsweetened || Kefir, water || Hemp milk, unsweetened || Coconut milk, lite, unsweetened || Coconut milk, full-fat, unsweetened || Almond milk, unsweetened

FATS AND OILS

POTENTIAL PRO-INFLAMMATORY INGREDIENTS (AVOID/MINIMIZE)

Vegetable oil || Sunflower oil || Soybean oil || Shortening || Sesame oil || Safflower oil || Peanut oil || Palm oil || Margarine || Lite olive oil || Hydrogenated oils || Corn oil || Canola oil || Butter

INGREDIENTS THAT REDUCE INFLAMMATION (EAT THESE)

Macadamia oil || Coconut oil || Avocado oil

POTENT ANTI-INFLAMMATORY FOODS (EAT A LOT)

Extra-Virgin Olive Oil

FRUITS

POTENTIAL PRO-INFLAMMATORY INGREDIENTS (AVOID/MINIMIZE)

Processed juices with added sugar || Canned fruit in syrup

INGREDIENTS THAT REDUCE INFLAMMATION (EAT THESE)

Yuzu || Watermelon || Ugli fruit || Tayberry || Tangerine || Tamarind || Strawberry || Star fruit || Satsuma || Santa Claus melon || Salmonberry || Red currant || Raspberry || Raisin || Quince || Prunes || Prickly pear || Pomelo || Pomegranate || Pluot || Plum || Plantain || Pineapple || Persimmon || Persian melon || Pear || Peach || Passionfruit || Papaya || Orange || Olives || Nectarine || Mulberry || Marionberry || Mangosteen || Mango || Mandarin || Lychee || Lime || Lemon || Kumquat || Kiwi || Jackfruit || Huckleberry || Horned melon || Honeydew || Guava || Grapefruit || Grape || Gooseberry || Goji berry || Galia (melon) || Fig || Elderberry || Durian || Dragon fruit || Date || Currant || Cranberry || Coconut || Clementine || Chokecherry || Cherry || Charentais (melon) || Casaba melon || Cantaloupe || Canary melon || Breadfruit || Boysenberry || Blood orange || Blackcurrant || Blackberry || Banana || Avocado || Asian pear || Apricot || Apple || Acai

POTENT ANTI-INFLAMMATORY FOODS (EAT A LOT)

Blueberries

GRAINS AND STARCHES

*INGREDIENTS THAT MAY
TRIGGER INFLAMMATION (AVOID/MINIMIZE)*

Wheat, refined || Rice, white || Potato starch || Pasta || Oatmeal, instant, with sugar || Flour, white || Cereal || Bread, white || Baked goods (bread, cookies, donuts, pies, etc.)

INGREDIENTS THAT REDUCE INFLAMMATION (EAT THESE)

Wild rice || Wheat, whole || Wheat, cracked || Teff || Rye || Rice, brown || Quinoa || Oats, rolled || Millet || Kamut || Farro || Cornstarch || Corn || Bulgur || Buckwheat || Barley || Arrowroot || Amaranth

MEATS, POULTRY, FISH, AND PROTEINS

POTENTIAL PRO-INFLAMMATORY INGREDIENTS (AVOID/MINIMIZE)

Whey protein || Trout, fried || Shrimp, fried || Scallops, fried || Sausage || Salami || Pork, ground || Liver (all types) || Lamb, rib chops || Lamb, rack || Kidney (all types) || Hot dogs || Heart (all types) || Ham || Gizzards || Foie gras || Fish, fried || Farmed seafood || Deli meats || Cured meats || Chicken, fried || Catfish, fried || Brains (all types) || Bologna || Beef, rib eye || Beef, prime rib || Beef, New York strip || Beef, feedlot || Bacon

INGREDIENTS THAT REDUCE INFLAMMATION (EAT THESE)

Venison || Turkey, free-range, skinless || Tilapia, wild-caught || Sturgeon, wild-caught || Snapper || Skate || Shrimp || Scallops || Razor clams || Pork, top loin roast || Pork, tenderloin (preferably pastured) || Pork, sirloin roast || Pork, rib chop || Pork, center loin chop || Pork, boneless top loin chop || Orange roughy || Mussels || Lamb, very lean cuts || Halibut || Elk || Eggs || Duck, free-range, skinless || Cod || Clams || Chicken, free-range, skinless || Catfish, wild-caught || Bison, lean || Beef, lean or very lean || Bass, wild-caught || Anchovy

POTENT ANTI-INFLAMMATORY FOODS (EAT A LOT)

Salmon (and other fatty fish including tuna, mackerel, sardines, and trout)

NUTS, SEEDS, AND LEGUMES

INGREDIENTS THAT REDUCE INFLAMMATION (EAT THESE)

Walnuts, raw || Sunflower seeds || Soybeans || Sesame seeds || Poppy seeds || Pistachios, raw || Pinto beans || Pine nuts || Pecans, raw || Peas, sugar snap || Peas, split || Peas, snow || Peas, green || Peas, black-eyed || Peanuts, raw || Peanut butter || Macadamia nuts, raw || Lima beans || Lentils || Kidney beans || Hazelnuts, raw || Flaxseed || Fava beans || Cocoa beans (dark chocolate, cocoa powder) || Chickpeas (garbanzo beans) || Chia seeds || Cashews, raw || Brazil nuts, raw || Black beans || Almonds, raw || Almond butter || Adzuki beans

POTENT ANTI-INFLAMMATORY FOODS (EAT A LOT)

NUTS

SWEETENERS

POTENTIAL PRO-INFLAMMATORY INGREDIENTS (AVOID/MINIMIZE)

Xylitol || Syrup, brown rice, corn, high fructose corn, maple (artificial), simple || Sugar, brown and powdered || Sugar alcohols || Sucralose (Splenda) || Sorbitol || Saccharine || Molasses, refined || Mannitol || Erythritol || Aspartame (NutraSweet) || Agave nectar || Acesulfame-K (Acesulfame potassium)

INGREDIENTS THAT REDUCE INFLAMMATION (EAT THESE)

Stevia || Maple syrup, pure || Honey

VEGETABLES

POTENTIAL PRO-INFLAMMATORY INGREDIENTS (AVOID/MINIMIZE)

Zucchini || Yam || Watercress || Water chestnut || Wakame || Turnip greens || Turnip || Tomatoes, canned (sugar-free) || Tomato sauce (sugar-free) || Tomatillo || Swiss chard || Sweet potato || Sunchoke || Sprouts || Spinach || Spaghetti squash || Shallots || Scallions || Rutabaga || Rapini || Purslane || Pumpkin || Potatoes || Pea pods || Pattypan squash || Parsnip || Onions || Okra || Nori || Nopales || Mustard greens || Mushrooms || Lettuce (all types) || Kohlrabi Leeks || Jicama

INGREDIENTS THAT REDUCE INFLAMMATION (EAT THESE)

Hearts of palm || Grape leaves || Frisée || Fennel || Endive || Eggplant || Edamame || Dulse || Cucumber || Corn || Collard greens || Chayote || Celery || Celeriac (celery root) || Cauliflower || Carrots || Cabbage || Butternut squash || Brussels sprouts || Broccolini || Broccoli rabe || Bok choy || Beets || Beet greens || Beans, green || Asparagus || Arugula || Artichoke || Acorn squash

POTENT ANTI-INFLAMMATORY FOODS (EAT A LOT)

Tomatoes || spinach || kale || broccoli || bell peppers

HERBS, AND SPICES

POTENTIAL PRO-INFLAMMATORY INGREDIENTS (AVOID/MINIMIZE)

Table salt || Spice blends with sugar || Seasoning salt || Garlic salt

INGREDIENTS THAT REDUCE INFLAMMATION (EAT THESE)

Vanilla bean || Thyme || Tarragon || Sumac || Spearmint || Salt, Himalayan pink and sea || Sage || Saffron || Rhubarb || Red pepper flakes || Radish || Radicchio || Pepper (black) || Parsley || Paprika || Oregano || Orange zest || Onion powder || Nutmeg || Mustard seed || Mustard powder || Mint || Marjoram || Mace || Lime zest || Lemongrass || Lemon zest || Lemon pepper || Lavender || Juniper berry || Horseradish || Herbes de Provence || Garam masala || Galangal || Fenugreek || Fennel seed || Dill || Curry powder || Cumin || Coriander || Cilantro || Chives || Chipotle || Chinese five-spice powder || Chile peppers || Chamomile || Celery salt || Cayenne || Cassia || Caraway || Bay leaves || Basil || Asafoetida || Anise, star || Anise || Allspice

POTENT ANTI-INFLAMMATORY FOODS (EAT A LOT)

TURMERIC || ROSEMARY || GINGER || GARLIC || CINNAMON

PANTRY ESSENTIALS

If you're serious about the anti-inflammatory diet, you will do well to make the following ingredients a staple in your pantry:

CANNED ITEMS

- Tomatoes, crushed
- Tomatoes, chopped
- Red bell peppers, roasted, in oil
- Coconut milk, lite
- Broth, vegetable, no salt added
- Broth, chicken, no salt added

HERBS AND SPICES

- Turmeric, ground
- Thyme, dried
- Salt, Himalayan pink or sea

- Rosemary, dried
- Red pepper flakes
- Peppercorns
- Oregano, dried
- Onion powder
- Nutmeg, ground
- Ginger, ground
- Garlic powder
- Curry powder
- Cinnamon, ground
- Chili powder

NUTS, SEEDS, LEGUMES, AND GRAINS

- Sunflower seeds
- Sesame seeds, toasted
- Rice, brown, cooked
- Quinoa
- Peanut butter
- Lentils, canned
- Chickpeas, canned
- Beans, kidney, canned
- Beans, black, canned
- Almond butter

OILS, VINEGARS, AND CONDIMENTS

- Vinegar, apple cider
- Soy sauce, low-sodium (or gluten-free or tamari)
- Olive oil, extra-virgin
- Mustard, Dijon

SUGAR, BAKING INGREDIENTS, AND FLOURS

- Vanilla extract
- Sugar, brown
- Stevia

- Milk, almond, hemp, or rice, unsweetened
- Maple syrup, pure
- Honey
- Green tea
- Cocoa powder, unsweetened
- Arrowroot powder (or cornstarch)

TIPS AND TRICKS

Here are a few suggestions I give to my clients to make it easier for them to cook the food, and stick to the diet:

- Weekly Diet Plans Work. If you think too much ahead, things will be hard. Plan for a week, or even less. Make a meal plan using the recipes in this book, and make a shopping list. Shopping only for the ingredients you'll be using in the following week will ensure that they stay fresh, and your brain stays relatively stress-free.
- Cook in Large Batches. If you're lazy like me and wouldn't like to cook three times every day, try cooking a LOT. This only works for dishes that store well in the fridge. Take a serving size out of the fridge, heat using a microwave, eat, repeat.
- Have Fun With Leftovers. Leftovers are a great opportunity to let your imagination run wild and invent a new recipe tailored to your personal taste!
- Veggies are Love. Buy lots of fresh vegetables when you're at a grocery store. Better yet, take a stroll through a farmers' market near you.
- Try Different Cooking Methods. Depending on how much time you have, and when you want to eat, a different cooking method might make the work easier. Slow cooking, for example, is great for someone who has a day job and would like to come back home to a home cooked meal, without another home cook.
- Prepare and Shop on Weekends and Holidays. If you have a full time job, make sure you take care of some of the planning and shopping on the day off.
- Frozen veggies and fruits are Great. There is a misconception that frozen fruits and vegetables lose their nutrition. That is just not true. These are usually flash frozen while they are at their peak of ripeness, and due to being frozen, that peak is maintained for much longer!
- Machine Tools are Handy. Food processors are love, Food processors are life.

- Store Food Right. Different ingredients like to be stored in different ways. While an ingredient is best stored in the freezer, another might do stored at room temperature. If you're not sure about the best way to store a particular ingredient, google is your friend!
- Internet for The Win. If you can't find that pesky ingredient in a nearby store, check online on amazon. If you can't figure out a cooking procedure by words alone, watch a YouTube video.

ABOUT THE RECIPES

All right! I think we are done with the basics. Let us dive into the recipes! Make sure you read the ingredients and directions carefully before starting a recipe. Make sure you're not allergic to any of the ingredients, and that you have all the tools used in the directions. Let's go!

SOUPS AND STEWS

ANTI-INFLAMMATORY SPRING PEA SOUP

Time To Prepare: five minutes

Time to Cook: fifteen minutes

Yield: Servings 6

Ingredients:

- ½ tsp. Black pepper powder
- ½ tsp. ground cumin
- 1 liter Vegetable stock
- 1 medium Chopped onion
- 2 tbsp. Coconut oil
- 2 tsp. Celtic sea salt
- 700 g. Fresh peas
- Chopped flat-leaf parsley
- Chopped mint leaves
- Fresh lemon juice
- Grated nutmeg
- Toasted sunflower seeds

Directions:

1. Warm the coconut oil in a pan set on moderate heat.
2. Mix in onions and stir fry for approximately five minutes.
3. Put in the stock and raise the heat. Throw in fresh peas and cook for five minutes. If you're using frozen peas, it should take half the time.
4. Pour in the lemon juice, salt, pepper, herbs, and spices. Stirring continuously
5. Remove the heat and allow it to cool before running it through a food processor to whatever consistency you prefer.
6. Serve with sunflower seed sprinkles and mint or parsley leaves.
7. Enjoy!

Nutritional Info: Calories: 115 kcal || Protein: 5 g || Fat: 5.91 g || Carbohydrates: 11.8 g

ANTI-INFLAMMATORY SWEET POTATO SOUP

Time To Prepare: twenty minutes

Time to Cook: thirty minutes

Yield: Servings 8

Ingredients:

- 1 13.66-ounce can lite coconut milk
- 1 big zucchini, cut width-wise
- 1 garlic clove
- 1 liter low-sodium vegetable stock
- 1 tablespoon sweet yellow curry powder
- 1 teaspoon black pepper
- 1 teaspoon cayenne pepper
- 1 teaspoon turmeric
- 1 white onion
- 2 moderate-sized white potatoes,
- 3 moderate-sized sweet potatoes,
- 3/4 tablespoons salt
- 4 cups of hot water
- 4 tablespoons olive oil
- A pinch of cinnamon
- A pinch of cloves

Directions:

1. Prepare every one of your vegetables by cutting, cleaning & cubing. Put in a safe spot.
2. To a large pot, include 4 tablespoons of additional virgin olive oil. Allow it to heat up swiftly; at that point, include your white onion. Allow it to sweat for minimum five minutes on low warmth.
3. Put in all your flavoring & garlic. Give it a decent mix; at that point, including the potatoes.
4. Allow these cook on moderate heat for around five minutes to get a pleasant darker shading. Continue blending to abstain from consuming.

5. Put in your stalk & water, warm it to the point of boiling & then stew for around 20-twenty-five minutes. Part of the way through the stewing procedure, include your zucchini.
6. After 20-twenty-five minutes, include your coconut milk. Before pouring the soup to the blender, do a fork content to guarantee your potatoes are cooked.
7. Use your blender to purée the soup. Embellishment with lemon juice, dark pepper & herbs & flavors of your preference.

Nutritional Info: Calories: 281 kcal || Protein: 4.1 g || Fat: 20.22 g || Carbohydrates: 23.8 g

BACON & CHEESE SOUP

Time To Prepare: fifteen minutes

Time to Cook: forty minutes

Yield: Servings 6

Ingredients:

- ½ cup sour cream, for serving
- ½ teaspoon cumin
- ½ teaspoon onion powder
- ½ teaspoon paprika
- 1 cup heavy cream
- 1 cup shredded cheddar cheese
- 1 pound of lean ground beef
- 1 tablespoon coconut oil, for cooking
- 1 teaspoon garlic powder
- 1 yellow onion, chopped
- 6 cups beef broth
- 6 slices uncured bacon

Directions:

1. Put in the coconut oil to a frying pan and cook the bacon until crunchy. Allow the bacon to cool and cut into little pieces. Set aside.
2. Once cooked, put in the lean ground beef to the same frying pan with the bacon fat and cook until browned.

3. Put in the onions and cook for an extra two to three minutes.
4. Put in all the ingredients minus the bacon, heavy cream, sour cream and cheese to a stockpot and stir. Cook for about twenty-five minutes.
5. Warm the heavy cream, and then put in the warmed cream and cheese and serve with the bacon and a spoonful of sour cream.

Nutritional Info: Calories: 498 || Carbohydrates: 5g || Fiber: 1g Net || Carbohydrates: 4g || Fat: 34g || Protein: 41g

BEEF AND VEGGIE SOUP

Time To Prepare: ten minutes

Time to Cook: twenty minutes

Yield: Servings 8

Ingredients:

- ½ cup heavy whipping cream
- ½ cup onion, chopped
- 1 (8 ounces / 227 g) package cream cheese, softened
- 1 pound (454 g) ground beef
- 1 tablespoon ground cumin
- 1 teaspoon chili powder
- 2 (10 ounces / 284 g) cans diced tomatoes and green chiles
- 2 (14.5 ounces / 411 g) cans beef broth
- 2 cloves garlic, minced
- 2 teaspoons salt, or to taste

Directions:

1. Position the ground beef, chopped onion, and garlic in a pot, stir until blended well. Cook on moderate to high heat for five to seven minutes or until the beef is thoroughly browned. Stir continuously.
2. Discard the grease extract from the beef, then put in chili powder and cumin, and cook for an extra two minutes. Stir continuously.

3. Put in the cream cheese to the pot and cook for three to five minutes more, then fold in the tomatoes and green chiles, beef broth, heavy whipping cream, and salt, and cook for about ten minutes to cook through. Keep stirring during the cooking.
4. Serve the soup in a big serving container. Allow to stand for a couple of minutes before you serve.

Nutritional Info: calories: 288 || total fat: 24g || carbs: 5.4g || protein: 13.4g || Cholesterol: 85mg || Sodium: 1310mg

BROCCOLI CHEDDAR & BACON SOUP

Time To Prepare: ten minutes

Time to Cook: ten minutes

Yield: Servings 6

Ingredients:

- ¼ teaspoon black pepper
- ½ teaspoon salt
- ½ white onion, chopped
- 1 cup broccoli florets finely chopped
- 1 cup heavy cream
- 1 cup shredded cheddar cheese
- 2 cloves garlic, chopped
- 2 cups chicken broth
- 3 slices cooked bacon, crumbled for serving

Directions:

1. Put in all the ingredients minus the heavy cream, cheddar cheese and bacon to a stockpot on moderate heat.
2. Heat to a simmer and cook for 5 minutes.
3. Warm the cream, and then put in the warm cream and cheddar cheese. Whisk until the desired smoothness is achieved.
4. Serve with crumbled bacon.

Nutritional Info: Calories: 220 || Carbohydrates: 4g || Fiber: 1g Net || Carbohydrates: 3g || Fat: 18g || Protein: 11g

---

BROCCOLI SOUP WITH GORGONZOLA CHEESE

Time To Prepare: ten minutes

Time to Cook: thirty minutes

Yield: Servings 4

Ingredients:

- ½ cup 18% cream
- 1 big broccoli, divided into little roses
- 1 flat teaspoon of sweet pepper
- 1 onion, diced
- 1 tablespoon of chopped fresh basil
- 1 tablespoon of chopped parsley
- 1 tablespoon of oil
- 150 g Gorgonzola cheese, diced
- 2 potatoes, peeled and diced
- 4 tablespoons of almond flakes roasted in a dry pan
- 5 garlic cloves, chopped
- 750 ml broth
- a pinch of sugar
- pumpkin oil (not necessary)
- salt and pepper

Directions:

1. In a big deep cooking pan, warm the oil on moderate heat, put the onion and garlic, and fry it until the vitrified glass onion.
2. Then put the broccoli with potatoes, pour the broth and cook for approximately fifteen-twenty minutes until the vegetables become tender. Put in basil, parsley, sugar, pepper, and pepper to taste.
3. Put in cheese and cream, and when the cheese dissolves, blend with a blender until the desired smoothness is achieved. Sprinkle with salt and pepper if required.

4. Serve the soup sprinkled with almond flakes and sprinkled with pumpkin oil.

Nutritional Info: Calories: 382 kcal ‖ Protein: 13.06 g ‖ Fat: 18.93 g ‖ Carbohydrates: 41.65 g

BROWN RICE AND SHITAKE MISO SOUP WITH SCALLION

Time To Prepare: ten minutes

Time to Cook: forty-five minutes

Yield: Servings 4

Ingredients:

- ½ teaspoon salt
- 1 (1½-inch) piece fresh ginger, peeled and cut
- 1 cup medium-grain brown rice
- 1 cup thinly cut shiitake mushroom caps
- 1 garlic clove, minced
- 1 tablespoon white miso
- 2 scallions, thinly cut
- 2 tablespoons finely chopped fresh cilantro
- 2 tablespoons sesame oil

Directions:

1. In a large pot, heat the oil on moderate to high heat.
2. Put in the mushrooms, garlic, and ginger and sauté until the mushrooms start to tenderize, approximately five minutes.
3. Place the rice and stir to uniformly coat with the oil.
4. Put in 2 cups of water and salt and place it to its boiling point.
5. Reduce the heat then cook until the rice is soft, thirty to forty minutes.
6. Use a little of the soup broth to tenderize the miso, then mix it into the pot until well mixed.
7. Stir in the scallions and cilantro, then serve.

Nutritional Info: Calories: 265 ‖ Total Fat: 8g ‖ Total Carbohydrates: 43g ‖ Sugar: 2g ‖ Fiber: 3g ‖ Protein: 5g ‖ Sodium: 456mg

BUFFALO SAUCE AND TURKEY SOUP

Time To Prepare: five minutes

Time to Cook: ten minutes

Yield: Servings 4

Ingredients:

- ⅓ cup buffalo sauce
- 2 cups turkey, cooked, shredded
- 3 tablespoons butter, melted
- 4 cups chicken broth
- 4 ounces (113 g) cream cheese
- 4 tablespoons cilantro, chopped
- From The Cupboard:
- Salt and freshly ground black pepper, to taste

Directions:

1. Place the buffalo sauce, cream cheese, and melted butter in a blender, and process until the desired smoothness is achieved.
2. Pour the buffalo sauce mixture in a deep cooking pan, and put in the chicken broth. Heat the soup using high heat until hot and nearly boil off but not boil. Keep stirring during the heating.
3. Put in the shredded turkey, and drizzle with salt and black pepper. Cook for five minutes or until the desired smoothness is achieved. Stir continuously.
4. Ladle the soup into a big container and top with chopped cilantro before you serve.

Nutritional Info: calories: 409 ‖ total fat: 29.7g ‖ net carbs: 9.2g ‖ protein: 26.4g

BUTTERNUT SQUASH SOUP WITH SHRIMP

Time To Prepare: ten minutes

Time to Cook: twenty minutes

Yield: Servings 4

Ingredients:

- ¼ cup slivered almonds (not necessary)
- ¼ teaspoon freshly ground black pepper
- 1 cup unsweetened almond milk
- 1 garlic clove, cut
- 1 pound cooked peeled shrimp, thawed if required
- 1 small red onion, finely chopped
- 1 teaspoon salt
- 1 teaspoon turmeric
- 2 cups peeled butternut squash cut into ¼-inch dice
- 2 tablespoons finely chopped fresh flat-leaf parsley
- 2 teaspoons grated or minced lemon zest
- 3 cups vegetable broth
- 3 tablespoons unsalted butter

Directions:

1. In a large pot, melt the butter on high heat.
2. Put in the onion, garlic, turmeric, salt, and pepper and sauté until the vegetables are tender and translucent, five to seven minutes.
3. Put in the broth and squash and bring to its boiling point.
4. Reduce the heat and cook until the squash has tenderized, approximately five minutes.
5. Put in the shrimp and almond milk and cook until thoroughly heated, approximately 2 minutes.
6. Drizzle with the almonds (if using), parsley, and lemon zest before you serve.

Nutritional Info: Calories: 275 ‖ Total Fat: 12g ‖ Total Carbohydrates: 12g ‖ Sugar: 3g ‖ Fiber: 2g; ‖ Protein: 30g ‖ Sodium: 1665mg

---

CANNELLINI BEAN SOUP

Time To Prepare: twenty-five minutes

Time to Cook: thirty minutes

Yield: Servings 6

Ingredients:

- 1 bunch red Swiss chard

- 1 cannellini beans
- 1 clove garlic (minced)
- 1 onion (chopped)
- 1 tablespoon extra-virgin olive oil
- 1/4 teaspoon nutmeg (grated)
- 1/8 teaspoon red pepper flakes (crushed)
- 2 ounces Parmesan cheese rind
- 2 slices smoked bacon (chopped)
- 2 tablespoons chopped sun-dried tomatoes
- 5 big sage leaves (minced)
- 5 leaves basil (chopped)
- 6 cups chicken broth

Directions:

1. Cook the bacon with garlic, onion, nutmeg, and red pepper flakes for five minutes.
2. Pour in beans, chicken broth, sun-dried tomatoes, and Parmesan cheese rind, simmering for about ten minutes.
3. Put in the cut chard and chard leaves into the soup.
4. Simmer and then put in into bowls with a sprinkle of oil and Parmesan cheese.

Nutritional Info: Calories: 215 kcal || Carbohydrates: 23 g || Fat: 10 g || Protein: 9.7 g

CARROT BROCCOLI STEW

Time To Prepare: ten minutes

Time to Cook: forty-five minutes

Yield: Servings 3

Ingredients:

- 1 cup Broccoli, florets
- 1 cup Carrots, cut
- 1 cup Heavy Cream
- 3 cups Chicken broth
- Salt and black pepper to taste

Directions:

1. Put in florets, cream, carrots, salt, and chicken broth; toss thoroughly. Secure the lid and cook on Meat/Stew mode for forty minutes on High. When ready, do a quick pressure release.
2. Move into serving bowls and drizzle black pepper on top.

Nutritional Info: Calories 145 || Protein: 1.5g || Carbs: 1.2g

---

CARROT, GINGER & TURMERIC SOUP

Time To Prepare: fifteen minutes

Time to Cook: forty minutes

Yield: Servings 8

Ingredients:

- ¼ cup full-fat unsweetened coconut milk
- ¾ pound carrots, peeled and chopped
- 1 sweet yellow onion, chopped
- 1 teaspoon ground turmeric
- 2 cloves garlic, chopped
- 2 teaspoons grated ginger
- 6 cups vegetable broth
- Pinch of sea salt & pepper, to taste

Directions:

1. Put in all the ingredients minus the coconut milk to a stockpot on moderate heat and bring to its boiling point. Reduce to a simmer and cook for forty minutes or until the carrots are soft.
2. Use an immersion blender and blend the soup until the desired smoothness is achieved. Mix in the coconut milk.
3. Enjoy immediately and freeze any remainings.

Nutritional Info: Calories: 73 || Carbohydrates: 7g || Fiber: 2g Net || Carbohydrates: 5g || Fat: 3g || Protein: 4g

CAULIFLOWER AND CLAM CHOWDER

Time To Prepare: ten minutes

Time to Cook: ten minutes

Yield: Servings 6

Ingredients:

- ½ teaspoon dried thyme
- 1 small yellow onion
- 1½ cups heavy whipping cream
- 3 (6.5-ounce / 184-g) cans chopped clams
- 3 tablespoons butter
- 4 cups chopped cauliflower
- From the cupboard:
- Salt and freshly ground black pepper, to taste

Directions:

1. Split the clams and clam juice into two bowls. Thin the clam juice with water to make 2 cups of juice.
2. Place the onion and butter in an instant pot and press the Sauté bottom, then sauté for a couple of minutes or until the onion is translucent.
3. Put in the clam juice and cauliflower into the instant pot. Place the lid on and press the Manual button, and set the temperature to 375ºF (190ºC), then cook for five minutes.
4. Quick Release the pressure, then open the lid and mix in the heavy cream and clams.
5. Push the Sauté bottom and cook for about three minutes or until the clams are opaque and firm, then drizzle with thyme, salt, and black pepper. Stir to mix thoroughly.
6. Ladle the chowder in a big container and serve warm.

Nutritional Info: calories: 252 || total fat: 17.3g || total carbs: 8.9g || fiber: 2.1g || net carbs: 6.8g || protein: 17.1g

CAULIFLOWER, COCONUT MILK, AND SHRIMP SOUP

Time To Prepare: five minutes

Time to Cook: 2 hours and fifteen minutes

Yield: Servings 4

Ingredients:

- 1 (13.5-ounce / 383-g) can unsweetened full-fat coconut milk
- 1 cup shrimp, peeled, deveined, tail off, and cooked
- 1 cup water
- 2 cups riced cauliflower
- 2 tablespoons chopped fresh cilantro leaves, divided
- 2 tablespoons red curry paste
- From the cupboard:
- Salt and freshly ground black pepper, to taste

Directions:

1. Put in the riced cauliflower, red curry paste, coconut milk, 1 tablespoon cilantro, water, then drizzle with salt and black pepper. Combine the mixture to blend well.
2. Place the slow cooker lid on and cook on HIGH for about two hours.
3. Place the shrimp on a clean working surface, then drizzle salt and black pepper to season.
4. Place the shrimp in the slow cooker and cook for fifteen minutes more.
5. Move the soup into a big container and top with the rest of the cilantro leaves before you serve.

Nutritional Info: calories: 268 || total fat: 21.3g || total carbs: 7.8g || fiber: 3.2g || net carbs: 4.6g || protein: 16.1g

CELERY SOUP

Time To Prepare: ten minutes

Time to Cook: twenty minutes

Yield: Servings 4

Ingredients:

- ½ cup brown onion, chopped
- ½ cup full-fat milk
- ½ pound with Salsiccia links, casing removed and cut
- ½ teaspoon dried chili flakes

- ½ teaspoon ground black pepper
- 1 carrot, chopped
- 1 garlic clove, pressed
- 2 teaspoon coconut oil
- 3 cups celery, chopped
- 3 cups roasted vegetable broth
- Kosher salt, to taste

Directions:

1. Simply throw all of the above ingredients into your Instant Pot; gently stir until blended.
2. Secure the lid. Choose "Soup/Broth" mode and High pressure; cook for about twenty-five minutes. Once cooking is complete, use a quick pressure release; cautiously remove the lid.
3. Ladle into four soup bowls and serve hot. Enjoy!

Nutritional Info: 150 Calories || 5.9g Fat || 5.9g Total Carbs || 16.4g Protein || 4.1g Sugars

---

CHEESY BROCCOLI SOUP

Time To Prepare: five minutes

Time to Cook: twenty minutes

Yield: Servings 4

Ingredients:

- 1 cup broccoli, cut into florets
- 1 cup chicken broth
- 1 cup heavy whipping cream
- 1 cup shredded Cheddar cheese, plus more for topping
- 2 tablespoons butter
- From the cupboard:
- Salt and freshly ground black pepper, to taste

Directions:

1. Place the butter in a deep cooking pan, and melt on moderate heat.
2. Put in and sauté the broccoli for four to five minutes or until tender.

3. Stir in the chicken broth and heavy whipping cream over the broccoli, and drizzle with salt and black pepper. Cook for approximately fifteen minutes or until the soup is smooth and thickened. Keep stirring during the cooking.
4. Lower the heat to low and gently fold in the Cheddar cheese. Keep stirring until well blended.
5. Ladle the soup into a big container. Spread more cheese over the soup before you serve.

Nutritional Info: calories: 386 ‖ total fat: 37.3g ‖ total carbs: 3.8g ‖ fiber: 1.1g ‖ net carbs: 2.7g ‖ protein: 9.8g

---

CHEESY CHICKEN SOUP

Time To Prepare: twenty minutes

Time to Cook: 33-40 minutes

Yield: Servings 6

Ingredients:

- ¼ teaspoon black pepper
- ½ cup shredded cheddar cheese
- ½ teaspoon cumin
- ½ teaspoon salt
- 1 cup whipped cream cheese
- 1 tablespoon coconut oil, for cooking
- 1 teaspoon chili powder
- 1 yellow onion, chopped
- 2 boneless, skinless chicken breasts
- 2 cloves garlic, chopped
- 2 cups chicken broth
- 2 cups water

Directions:

1. Heat a big frying pan on moderate heat with a ½ tablespoon of the coconut oil.
2. Brown the chicken breasts until thoroughly cooked. Set aside.

3. Put in the garlic and onion to a big stockpot with the rest of the 1 tablespoon of the coconut oil and sauté until translucent over low to moderate heat. This should take about three to five minutes.
4. Put in this chicken broth and water.
5. Whisk in the cream cheese and keep whisking over low to moderate heat until blended.
6. Put in in the spices and bring to its boiling point.
7. While the water is boiling, chop the chicken into bite-sized pieces and put in to the stockpot.
8. Reduce to a simmer and cook for half an hour.
9. Mix in the cheddar cheese before you serve.

Nutritional Info: Calories: 157 || Carbohydrates: 5g || Fiber: 1g Net || Carbohydrates: 4g || Fat: 7g || Protein: 17g

---

CHEESY TOMATO AND BASIL SOUP

Time To Prepare: five minutes

Time to Cook: fifteen minutes

Yield: Servings 12

Ingredients:

- ¼ teaspoon ground black pepper
- 1 tablespoon dried basil
- 1 teaspoon dried oregano
- 1 teaspoon salt
- 2 (14 ounces / 397 g) canned whole tomatoes, diced
- 2 garlic cloves, minced
- 2 tablespoons coconut oil
- 4 cups chicken broth
- 4 ounces (113 g) red onions, finely diced
- 5 ounces (142 g) grated Parmesan cheese, plus more for decoration
- 8 ounces (227 g) cream cheese, softened
- Fresh basil, chopped, for decoration

Directions:

1. Grease a nonstick frying pan with coconut oil, and sauté the onions, basil, oregano, and garlic in the frying pan for about four minutes or until aromatic.
2. Put in the cream cheese and fully whisk until no clump, then fold in the chicken broth, and put in the cheese, tomatoes, salt, and pepper. Stir to blend well.
3. Cover the lid and bring them to a simmer on moderate heat for eight minutes. Move the soup into a blender, then blitz until it becomes thick.
4. Lightly pour the soup into a big serving container and sprinkle with Parmesan cheese and basil as decorate.

Nutritional Info: calories: 146 || total fat: 12g || net carbs: 3g || fiber: 1g || protein: 6g

CHICKEN AND CAULIFLOWER CURRY STEW

Time To Prepare: fifteen minutes

Time to Cook: 4 hours

Yield: Servings 7

Ingredients:

- ¼ cup fresh cilantro, chopped
- ⅓ cup coconut oil
- 1 green bell pepper, chopped
- 1 pound (454 g) cauliflower, chopped into little pieces
- 1.5pounds (680 g) skinless, boneless chicken thighs, cut into bite-sized pieces
- 14 ounces (397 g) unsweetened coconut milk
- 2 tablespoons curry powder
- 2 tablespoons ginger garlic paste
- Salt and ground black pepper, to taste

Directions:

1. Warm half of the coconut oil in a nonstick frying pan on moderate heat, then sauté the garlic ginger paste and curry powder for a minutes or until aromatic.
2. Put in the chicken pieces, and drizzle with salt and pepper. sauté for another ten minutes or until the chicken is mildly browned. Remove from the frying pan and set aside in warm.

3. Warm another half of coconut oil in the frying pan, then sauté the cauliflower and bell pepper on moderate to high heat for one to two minutes.
4. Then fold in the coconut milk and reduce the heat to low. Cover with lid and stew for about forty-five minutes.
5. Drizzle with salt and pepper, then put in the sautéed chicken. Move the stew to a big platter and serve with cilantro on top as decorate.

Nutritional Info: calories: 782 || total fat: 68g || net carbs: 9g || fiber: 5g || protein: 33g

CHICKEN AND KALE SOUP

Time To Prepare: five minutes

Time to Cook: 4 hours

Yield: Servings 4

Ingredients:

- 1 (7-ounce / 198-g) bunch kale, trimmed and chopped
- 1 big chicken breast, cut into little strips
- 2 tablespoons olive oil
- 3 tablespoons fresh ginger, grated
- 6 cups chicken stock
- 6 garlic cloves, finely chopped
- From the cupboard:
- Salt and freshly ground black pepper, to taste

Directions:

1. Grease the insert of the slow cooker with olive oil.
2. Combine the chicken breast, stock, kale, ginger, garlic, ginger, salt, and black pepper in the slow cooker.
3. Place the slow cooker lid on and cook on HIGH for 4 hours.
4. Ladle the stew in a big container and serve warm.

Nutritional Info: calories: 168 || total fat: 7.6g || total carbs: 8.3g || fiber: 2.1g || net carbs: 6.2g || protein: 18.7g

CHICKEN CHILI BLANCO

Time To Prepare: ten minutes

Time to Cook: twenty minutes

Yield: Servings 4

Ingredients:

- ¼ teaspoon cayenne pepper
- 1 tablespoon ghee
- 1 teaspoon chili powder
- 2 (4-ounce) cans diced mild green chiles with their liquid
- 2 scallions, cut
- 2 small onions, chopped
- 2 teaspoons dried oregano
- 4 cups chicken broth or vegetable broth
- 4 cups shredded cooked chicken
- 4 cups white beans, drained and washed well
- 4 teaspoons ground cumin
- 6 garlic cloves, minced

Directions:

1. In a huge soup pot on moderate heat, melt the ghee.
2. Put in the onions and garlic, and sauté for five minutes.
3. Place the chiles, and cook for a couple of minutes, stirring.
4. Mix in the beans, broth, cumin, oregano, chili powder, and cayenne pepper. Heat it until it simmers.
5. Put in the chicken, bring to a simmer, decrease the heat to moderate-low, and cook for about ten minutes. Serve instantly, sprinkled with the scallions.

Nutritional Info: Calories: 304 ‖ Total Fat: 4g ‖ Saturated Fat: 2g ‖ Cholesterol: 0mg ‖ Carbohydrates: 46g ‖ Fiber: 12g ‖ Protein: 21g

CHICKEN TORTILLA SOUP

Time To Prepare: ten minutes

Time to Cook: twenty minutes

Yield: Servings 8-10

Ingredients:

- 1 teaspoon cayenne pepper or to taste
- 2 cups onions, chopped
- 2 teaspoons chili powder
- 2 teaspoons cumin powder
- 2 teaspoons dried oregano
- 2 teaspoons garlic powder
- 4 cups carrots, cut
- 4 cups celery, cut
- 4 cups water
- 4 teaspoons olive oil
- 6 cups rotisserie chicken, skinless, chopped or shredded
- 8 cloves garlic, minced
- 8 cups chicken broth
- 8 medium tomatoes, chopped
- Avocado, peeled, pitted, chopped
- For the topping: Use any (not necessary)
- Fresh cilantro, chopped
- Greek yogurt
- Pepper powder to taste
- Salt to taste
- Tortilla chips, crumbled

Directions:

1. Put a soup pot on moderate heat. Put in oil.
2. When the oil is warmed, put the onion and celery and sauté until slightly soft.
3. Put in garlic and sauté for a few seconds until aromatic. Stir in the tomatoes and cook until tender. Remove the heat.
4. Move into a blender. Put in water and blend until the desired smoothness is achieved.
5. Put back the mixed mixture into the pot. Put in the remaining ingredients and stir.
6. If it's beginning to boil, reduce the heat then simmer until vegetables are tender.

7. Ladle into soup bowls before you serve.

Nutritional Info: Calories: 1593 kcal ‖ Protein: 147.22 g ‖ Fat: 102.27 g ‖ Carbohydrates: 13.17 g

CHICKPEA CURRY SOUP

Time To Prepare: ten minutes

Time to Cook: twenty-five minutes

Yield: Servings 4

Ingredients:

- ¼ cup extra-virgin olive oil or coconut oil
- 1 (fifteen-ounce) can chickpeas, drained and washed
- 1 big apple, cored, peeled, and slice into ¼-inch dice
- 1 cup full-fat coconut milk
- 1 medium onion, finely chopped
- 1 teaspoon salt
- 2 garlic cloves, cut
- 2 tablespoons finely chopped fresh cilantro
- 2 teaspoons curry powder
- 3 cups peeled butternut squash cut into ½-inch dice
- 3 cups vegetable broth

Directions:

1. In a large pot, heat the oil on high heat.
2. Put in the onion and garlic and sauté until the onion starts to brown, six to eight minutes.
3. Place the apple, curry powder, and salt and sauté to toast the curry powder, one to two minutes.
4. Place the squash and broth then bring to its boiling point.
5. Reduce the heat then cook until the squash is soft about ten minutes.
6. Mix in the coconut milk.
7. Use an immersion blender to purée the soup in the pot until the desired smoothness is achieved.
8. Mix in the chickpeas and cilantro, heat through for one to two minutes, before you serve.

Nutritional Info: Calories: 469 || Total Fat: 30g || Total Carbohydrates: 45g || Sugar: 14g || Fiber: 10g || Protein: 12g || Sodium: 1174mg

---

CLEAR CLAM CHOWDER

Time To Prepare: ten minutes

Time to Cook: fifteen minutes

Yield: Servings 4

Ingredients:

- ¼ teaspoon freshly ground black pepper
- ½ teaspoon dried thyme
- ½ teaspoon salt
- 1 (10-ounce) can clams
- 1 (8-ounce) bottle clam juice
- 1 small red onion, cut into ¼-inch dice
- 2 celery stalks, thinly cut
- 2 cups vegetable broth
- 2 garlic cloves, cut
- 2 medium carrots, cut into ½-inch pieces
- 2 tablespoons unsalted butter

Directions:

1. In a large pot, melt the butter on high heat.
2. Put in the carrots, celery, onion, and garlic and sauté until slightly softened two to three minutes.
3. Pour the broth and clam juice, then bring it to its boiling point.
4. Reduce the heat and cook until the carrots are soft, three to five minutes.
5. Mix in the clams and their juices, thyme, salt, and pepper, heat through for two to three minutes, before you serve.

Nutritional Info: Calories: 156 || Total Fat: 7g || Total Carbohydrates: 7g || Sugar: 3g || Fiber: 1g || Protein: 14g || Sodium: 981mg

COCONUT CASHEW SOUP WITH BUTTERNUT SQUASH

Time To Prepare: ten minutes

Time to Cook: twenty minutes

Yield: Servings 6

Ingredients:

- ½ tsp. salt
- ¾ cup toasted cashews
- 1 (14-ounce) can full-fat coconut milk
- 1 cup mung bean sprouts
- 1 small butternut squash, halved, diced
- 1 small Napa cabbage, shredded
- 1 white onion, diced
- 1½ tbsp. Ginger, peeled and minced
- 2 carrots, chopped
- 2 cups green beans, trimmed
- 2 red chili peppers, seeded and diced
- 2 tbsp. coconut oil
- 3 cups vegetable broth
- 3 garlic cloves, peeled and minced
- 4 tablespoons toasted coconut shavings
- Freshly ground black pepper

Directions:

1. In a huge soup pot on moderate heat, melt the coconut oil.
2. Place the cashews and sauté for a couple of minutes. Take off from the pan and save for later.
3. Place the peppers, garlic, and onion, and sauté for minimum 6 minutes. Then put the ginger and carrots, and sauté for minimum 3 minutes, or until the carrots and squash start to become tender.
4. Stir in the cabbage, green beans, broth, coconut milk, and salt, flavor with pepper. Simmer for fifteen minutes. Remove the heat.
5. Mix in the bean sprouts and coconut shavings.

6. Pour into soup bowls and serve instantly.

Nutritional Info: Calories: 340 || Total Fat: 25g || Saturated Fat: 20g || Cholesterol: 0mg || Carbohydrates: 23g || Fiber: 5g || Protein: 7g

---

COCONUT CURRIED BAN-APPLE SOUP

Time To Prepare: ten minutes

Time to Cook: 10-fifteen minutes

Yield: Servings 4

Ingredients:

- ¼ cup toasted coconut, for decoration
- 1 big potato 1 Granny Smith apple
- 1 celery heart
- 1 cup coconut milk
- 1 ripe banana
- 1 sweet onion
- 1 teaspoon curry powder
- 1 teaspoon salt
- 2 cups Basic Vegetable Stock or low-sodium canned vegetable stock
- 2 tablespoons chopped fresh cilantro, for decoration

Directions:

1. Place the vegetable stock in a soup pot.
2. Peel the banana and potato, cut them, and place them in the soup pot. Core the apple, cut it, and put in it to the soup pot. Cut the celery heart and onion and put in them to the soup pot.
3. Put the soup to its boiling point, then reduce the heat and simmer for ten to fifteen minutes. Put in the coconut milk, curry powder, and salt.
4. Place the hot soup in a blender and purée.
5. Serve the soup hot. Decorate using toasted coconut and cilantro.

Nutritional Info: Calories: 344 || Fat: 19 g || Protein: 6 g || Sodium: 886 mg || Fiber: 7 g || Carbohydrates: 40 g

CREAM OF MUSHROOM SOUP

Time To Prepare: twenty minutes

Time to Cook: thirty minutes

Yield: Servings 6

Ingredients:

- 5 cups mushrooms (cut)
- 1 tablespoon sherry
- 3 tablespoons butter
- 3 tablespoons flour
- 1 cup half-and-half
- Salt
- Ground black pepper
- 1½ cups chicken broth
- ½ cup onion (chopped)
- 1/8 teaspoon dried thyme

Directions:

1. Cook mushrooms with onion and thyme in the broth until soft.
2. Puree the mixture.
3. Whisk some flour in a pan of melted butter. Put in half-and-half, vegetable puree, and seasoning. Boil until it becomes thick.
4. Put in sherry.

Nutritional Info: Calories: 148 kcal || Carbohydrates: 8.6 g || Fat: 11 g || Protein: 4 g

CREAMY & CULTURE TOMATO SAUCE

Time To Prepare: ten minutes

Time to Cook: fifteen-twenty minutes

Yield: Servings 6

Ingredients:

- ⅛ teaspoon dried thyme

- ⅛ teaspoon freshly ground black pepper
- ¼ cup tomato paste
- ¼ teaspoon chili powder
- ½ cup plain whole-milk yogurt
- ½ teaspoon salt
- 1 small onion, chopped
- 1 tablespoon ghee
- 1 teaspoon dried basil
- 1 teaspoon dried oregano
- 2 (14-ounce) cans diced tomatoes with their juice
- 2 cups vegetable broth
- 3 garlic cloves, chopped

Directions:

1. In a huge soup pot on moderate heat, melt the ghee.
2. Place the onion and garlic, and sauté for five minutes.
3. Stir in the basil, oregano, salt, chili powder, pepper, and thyme.
4. Place the tomatoes, broth, and tomato paste, and stir until blended. Heat to a simmer, turn the heat to low, and cook for five to ten minutes. Take away the pot from the heat. With an immersion blender (or in batches in a standard blender), purée the mixture in the pot until you have the desired consistency.
5. Put in the yogurt. Blend for a minute more. Serve instantly.

Nutritional Info: Calories: 157 || Total Fat: 6g || Saturated Fat: 3g || Cholesterol: 3mg || Carbohydrates: 25g || Fiber: 13g || Protein: 8g

---

CREAMY BROCCOLI SOUP

Time To Prepare: fifteen minutes

Time to Cook: 4 hours

Yield: Servings 7

Ingredients:

- ¼ teaspoon ground black pepper
- ½ teaspoon paprika powder

- ½ teaspoon salt
- ⅔ cup heavy whipping cream
- 1 pinch cayenne pepper
- 1 red onion, roughly chopped
- 1 tablespoon olive oil
- 2 cups chicken broth
- 20 ounces (567 g) broccoli, cut into stalks and florets
- 3 garlic cloves, chopped
- 3 tablespoons butter
- ounces (99 g) Cheddar cheese, shredded

Directions:

1. Warm 1 tablespoon of butter and olive oil in a deep cooking pan, then fry the broccoli stalks and chopped onion on moderate heat for five minutes until soft.
2. Put in the garlic and keep frying for a couple of minutes until mildly browned, then drizzle with cayenne pepper, paprika, salt, and ground black pepper. Cook for another one minutes.
3. Pour over the chicken broth. Cover the lid and leave to simmer for five minutes.
4. Take away the cooked vegetables from the deep cooking pan to a food processor and process. Lightly ladle the soup into the food processor while processing until creamy.
5. Melt the rest of the butter in the deep cooking pan, and fry the broccoli florets for five minutes until tender and soft.
6. Pour the soup from the food processor into the deep cooking pan. Blend to mix thoroughly. If the soup is too thick, you can put in some water to make it thinner.
7. Bring the soup to its boiling point, then reduce the heat and bring to a simmer using low heat for about three minutes.
8. Put in the Cheddar cheese and heavy whipping cream and cook for a couple of minutes more until the cheese melts.
9. Take away the soup from the deep cooking pan and serve warm.

Nutritional Info: calories: 266 || total fat: 23g || net carbs: 7g || fiber: 3g || protein: 8g

CREAMY CELERY AND CHICKEN BROTH

Time To Prepare: five minutes

Time to Cook: twenty minutes

Yield: Servings 4

Ingredients:

- ¼ cup celery, chopped
- ½ cup coconut cream
- 1 onion, chopped
- 2 chicken breasts, chopped
- 3 tablespoons butter
- 4 cups water
- From The Cupboard:
- Salt and freshly ground black pepper, to taste

Directions:

1. Place the butter in a deep cooking pan, and melt on moderate heat.
2. Put in and sauté the celery and onion for about three minutes or until the onion is translucent.
3. Put in the chicken, salt, black pepper, and water, and simmer for fifteen minutes. Keep stirring during the simmering.
4. Mix in the coconut cream. Pour the soup in a big container and serve warm.

Nutritional Info: calories: 398 ‖ total fat: 24.4g ‖ net carbs: 5.9g ‖ protein: 29.3g

---

CREAMY LEEK SOUP

Time To Prepare: two minutes

Time to Cook: 8 minutes

Yield: Servings 4

Ingredients:

- ½ cup heavy cream
- ½ cup Monterey-Jack cheese, shredded
- ½ cup tomato purée
- ½ pound chorizo, cut

- 1 bay leaf
- 1 cup leeks, chopped
- 1 green chili, deseeded and finely chopped
- 1 tablespoon sesame oil
- 2 chicken bouillon cubes
- 2 cloves garlic, minced
- 4 cups water

Directions:

1. Push the "Sauté" button to heat up your Instant Pot. Once hot, heat the oil and sauté the leeks until soft.
2. Now, mix in chorizo, garlic, and green chili; carry on cooking until aromatic. Next, put in water, tomato puree, heavy cream, bouillon cubes, and bay leaf.
3. Secure the lid. Choose "Manual" mode and High pressure; cook for about six minutes. Once cooking is complete, use a natural pressure release; cautiously remove the lid.
4. Next, press the "Sauté" button and put in the cheese; allow it to simmer until the cheese is melted and thoroughly heated.

Nutritional Info: 428 Calories || 36g Fat || 6.1g Total Carbs || 18.9g Protein || 2.1g Sugars

---

CREAMY PARSNIP SOUP

Time To Prepare: twenty-five minutes

Time to Cook: 60 minutes

Yield: Servings 10

Ingredients:

- 1 big onion (diced)
- 1 cup whole milk
- 1 tablespoon brown sugar
- 1 tablespoon butter
- 1 tablespoon olive oil
- 1 teaspoon ground ginger
- ½ teaspoon ground allspice
- ½ teaspoon ground cardamom

- ½ teaspoon ground nutmeg
- 1/4 teaspoon cayenne pepper
- 2 pounds parsnips (peeled, cut)
- 3 carrots (peeled, cut)
- 3 cloves garlic (minced)
- 3 stalks celery (diced)
- 4 cups chicken stock
- Ground black pepper
- Salt

Directions:

1. Preheat your oven to 425 F.
2. Toss the parsnips and carrots with oil and seasoning in a container. Put them over a baking sheet.
3. Roast in oven until for half an hour
4. Cook the onion and celery in oil till golden brown, approximately seven minutes. Put in butter, brown sugar, garlic, and the parsnips and carrots, cooking for about ten minutes.
5. Season and stir. Put in the chicken stock to its boiling point until soft.
6. Puree the soup.
7. Put in milk and cream and simmer some more before you serve with seasoning.

Nutritional Info: Calories: 187 kcal ‖ Carbohydrates: 24 g ‖ Fat: 9 g ‖ Protein: 3 g

---

CREAMY PUMPKIN PUREE SOUP

Time To Prepare: ten minutes

Time to Cook: forty-five minutes

Yield: Servings 3

Ingredients:

- 1 cup Heavy Cream
- 1 cup Pumpkin puree
- 2 cups Chicken broth
- 2 tbsp. Olive oil
- 4-5 Garlic cloves

- Salt and black pepper to taste

Directions:

1. In the Instant Pot, put in all ingredients.
2. Secure the lid and cook for forty minutes on Meat/Stew mode on High. When ready, press Cancel and do a quick pressure release.
3. Move to a blender and blend thoroughly. Pour into serving bowls to serve.

Nutritional Info: Calories 465 || Protein: 15.4g || Carbs: 6.2g || Fat: 43.5g

CREAMY TURKEY SOUP

Time To Prepare: fifteen minutes

Time to Cook: 4 hours

Yield: Servings 7

Ingredients:

- 1 carrot, chopped
- 1 cup cream cheese
- 1 pound turkey breast, cubed
- 1 stalk celery, chopped
- 1 teaspoon freshly chopped rosemary
- 3 cloves garlic, chopped
- 5 cups chicken broth
- Salt & black pepper, to taste

Directions:

1. Put in all the ingredients minus the cream cheese to the base of a slow cooker.
2. Cook on high for 4 hours.
3. Mix in the cream cheese until well blended.

Nutritional Info: Calories: 216 || Carbohydrates: 6g || Fiber: 1g Net || Carbohydrates: 5g || Fat: 14g || Protein: 17g

CREAMY TURMERIC CAULIFLOWER SOUP

Time To Prepare: ten minutes

Time to Cook: fifteen minutes

Yield: Servings 4

Ingredients:

- ¼ cup finely chopped fresh cilantro
- ¼ teaspoon freshly ground black pepper
- ¼ teaspoon ground cumin
- ½ teaspoon salt
- 1 (1¼-inch) piece fresh ginger, peeled and cut
- 1 cup full-fat coconut milk
- 1 garlic clove, peeled
- 1 leek, white part only, thinly cut
- 1½ teaspoons turmeric
- 2 tablespoons extra-virgin olive oil
- 3 cups cauliflower florets
- 3 cups vegetable broth

Directions:

1. In a large pot, heat the oil on high heat.
2. Put in the leek, and sauté until it just starts to brown, three to four minutes.
3. Put in the cauliflower, garlic, ginger, turmeric, salt, pepper, and cumin and sauté to lightly toast the spices, one to two minutes.
4. Pour the broth then bring to its boiling point.
5. Reduce the heat and cook until the cauliflower is soft about five minutes.
6. Use an immersion blender to purée the soup in the pot until the desired smoothness is achieved.
7. Stir in the coconut milk and cilantro, heat through, before you serve.

Nutritional Info: Calories: 264 || Total Fat: 23g || Total Carbohydrates: 12g || Sugar: 5g || Fiber: 4g || Protein: 7g || Sodium: 900mg

---

CROCK-POT TURKEY TACO SOUP

Time To Prepare: ten minutes

Time to Cook: 4 hours

Yield: Servings 6

Ingredients:

- 1 cup canned diced tomatoes (no sugar added)
- 1 cup whipped cream cheese
- 1 pound ground turkey
- 1 tablespoon chili powder
- 1 teaspoon cumin
- 1 teaspoon garlic powder
- 1 teaspoon onion powder
- 1 yellow onion, chopped
- 5 cups chicken bone broth (you can also use regular chicken broth)

Directions:

1. Put in all the ingredients to the base of a Crock-Pot minus the cream cheese and cover with the chicken broth.
2. Set on high and cook for 4 hours putting in in the cream cheese at the 3.5 hour mark.
3. Stir thoroughly before you serve.

Nutritional Info: Calories: 335|| Carbohydrates: 6g|| Fiber: 1gNet || Carbohydrates: 5g|| Fat: 23g|| Protein: 28g

---

DETOX CABBAGE SOUP

Time To Prepare: ten minutes

Time to Cook: thirty-five minutes

Yield: Servings 4

Ingredients:

- 1 tbs. freshly grated ginger root
- 2 big carrot
- 1 cup whole canned tomatoes with juice
- 1 whole head of cabbage

- 1 tbs. freshly grated turmeric root
- 3 celery stalks with leaves
- Enough water to immerse the vegetables
- 2 medium Russet potatoes
- Sea salt & black pepper to taste
- ½ medium onion
- 1/4 cup extra virgin olive oil

Directions:

1. Heat the oil in a large pot on moderate heat for a couple of minutes.
2. Put in the celery, onions, ginger, carrots & turmeric, then sauté on medium until translucent. Sprinkle with salt & pepper to taste.
3. With the heat still on moderate, dice the potatoes & generally slash the cabbage at that point put in to the pot alongside the whole tomatoes & juice.
4. While they cook, break separated the tomatoes using a fork or blade. Fill the pot with sufficient water to simply cover the cabbage.
5. Cover with a top & heat to the point of boiling. When bubbling, evacuate the top & cook for around thirty minutes or until the potatoes & cabbage are fork delicate. Put in the ice chest for as long as 5 days & in the cooler for as long as three months.

Nutritional Info: Calories: 359 kcal **||** Protein: 10.85 g **||** Fat: 12.68 g **||** Carbohydrates: 54.94 g

---

FENNEL AND PEAR SOUP

Time To Prepare: fifteen minutes

Time to Cook: twenty minutes

Yield: Servings 4

Ingredients:

- ⅛ Teaspoon ground nutmeg
- ¼ cup freshly squeezed lemon juice
- ¼ cup honey
- ¼ teaspoon freshly ground black pepper
- 1 teaspoon finely chopped fresh tarragon
- 1 teaspoon salt

- 2 fennel bulbs, trimmed and slice into ½-inch dice
- 2 shallots, halved
- 2 tablespoons extra-virgin olive oil
- 4 cups vegetable broth
- 4 pears, cored and slice into ½-inch dice

Directions:

1. In a large pot, heat the oil on high heat.
2. Put in the pears, fennel, and shallots, and sauté until the pears and fennel barely start to brown, approximately five minutes.
3. Pour the broth, then bring to its boiling point.
4. Reduce the heat to a simmer, then cook, once in a while stirring, until the fennel is soft, 5 to 8 minutes.
5. Stir in the lemon juice, honey, salt, pepper, and nutmeg.
6. Use an immersion blender to purée the soup in the pot until the desired smoothness is achieved.
7. Drizzle with the tarragon before you serve.

Nutritional Info: Calories: 328 || Total Fat: 9g || Total Carbohydrates: 60g || Sugar: 39g || Fiber: 10g || Protein: 7g || Sodium: 1413mg

FRENCH CARAMELIZED ONION SOUP

Time To Prepare: five minutes

Time to Cook: ten minutes

Yield: Servings 4

Ingredients:

- ½ stick butter, softened
- 4 cups chicken stock
- ½ teaspoon dried basil
- Kosher salt and ground black pepper, to taste
- ½ cup Swiss cheese, freshly grated
- 3/4 pound yellow onions, cut

Directions:

1. Push the "Sauté" button to heat up your Instant Pot. Once hot, melt the butter and sauté the onions until caramelized and soft.
2. Put in chicken stock, basil, salt, and black pepper.
3. Secure the lid. Choose "Manual" mode and High pressure; cook for about ten minutes. Once cooking is complete, use a quick pressure release; cautiously remove the lid.
4. Ladle the soup into separate bowls and top with grated cheese. Enjoy!

Nutritional Info: 228 Calories ‖ 18g Fat ‖ 5.3g Total Carbs ‖ 10.5g Protein ‖ 3.5g Sugars

---

GARLIC AND LENTIL SOUP

Time To Prepare: fifteen minutes

Time to Cook: fifteen minutes

Yield: Servings 4

Ingredients:

- ¼ cup chopped walnuts (not necessary)
- ¼ teaspoon freshly ground black pepper
- 1 (fifteen-ounce) can lentils, drained and washed
- 1 small white onion, cut into ¼-inch dice
- 1 tablespoon minced or grated orange zest
- 1 teaspoon ground cinnamon
- 1 teaspoon salt
- 2 garlic cloves, thinly cut
- 2 medium carrots, thinly cut
- 2 tablespoons extra-virgin olive oil
- 2 tablespoons finely chopped fresh flat-leaf parsley
- 3 cups vegetable broth

Directions:

1. In a large pot, heat the oil using high heat.
2. Put in the carrots, onion, and garlic and sauté until tender, five to seven minutes.

3. Place the cinnamon, salt, and pepper and stir to uniformly coat the vegetables, one to two minutes.
4. Pour the broth then bring to its boiling point.
5. Reduce the heat to a simmer, put in the lentils and cook until they are thoroughly heated about one minute.
6. Mix in the orange zest and serve, sprinkled with the walnuts (if using) and parsley.

Nutritional Info: Calories: 201 || Total Fat: 8g || Total Carbohydrates 22g || Sugar: 4g || Fiber: 8g || Protein: 11g || Sodium: 1178mg

GARLIC MUSHROOM & BEEF SOUP

Time To Prepare: ten minutes

Time to Cook: forty minutes

Yield: Servings 6

Ingredients:

- ½ cup heavy cream
- ½ cup whipped cream cheese
- 1 pound beef chuck, cubed
- 1 tablespoon coconut oil, for cooking
- 1 yellow onion, chopped
- 1½ cups cremini mushrooms
- 2 cloves garlic, chopped
- 6 cups beef broth
- Salt & pepper, to taste

Directions:

1. Put in the coconut oil to a frying pan and brown the beef.
2. Once cooked, put in the beef to the base of a stockpot with all of the ingredients minus the heavy cream. Mix thoroughly.
3. Heat to a simmer and whisk again until the cream cheese is mixed uniformly into the soup.
4. Cook for half an hour
5. Warm the heavy cream, and then put in to the soup.

Nutritional Info: Calories: 315|| Carbohydrates: 5g|| Fiber: 1gNet || Carbohydrates: 4g|| Fat: 19g|| Protein: 30g

---

GARLICKY CHICKEN SOUP

Time To Prepare: ten minutes

Time to Cook: fifteen minutes

Yield: Servings 6

Ingredients:

- ¼ teaspoon black pepper
- ½ cup whipped cream cheese
- 1 tablespoon butter for cooking
- 1 teaspoon salt
- 1 teaspoon thyme
- 2 boneless, skinless chicken breasts
- 3 cloves garlic, chopped
- 4 cups chicken broth

Directions:

1. Preheat a stockpot on moderate heat with the butter.
2. Put in the chicken and brown until completely thoroughly cooked. Turn off the heat.
3. Shred the chicken and put in it back to the stockpot together with the rest of the ingredients minus the cream cheese.
4. Heat to a simmer.
5. Put in in the cream cheese and whisk until there are no more clumps.
6. Simmer for about ten minutes before you serve.

Nutritional Info: Calories: 128 || Carbohydrates: 2g || Fiber: 0g Net || Carbohydrates: 2g || Fat: 6g || Protein: 16g

---

GOLDEN CHICKPEA AND VEGETABLE SOUP

Time To Prepare: fifteen minutes

Time to Cook: twenty minutes

Yield: Servings 6

Ingredients:

- 1 ½ cup Diced celery
- 1 ½ cup Sliced leeks
- 1 cup cooked chickpeas
- 1 cup diced carrots
- 1 cup Torn curly kale leaves
- 1 tbsp. Grated ginger
- 2 cloves minced garlic
- 2 cups Cauliflower florets
- 2 tbsp. Curry powder
- 2 tbsp. Minced organic parsley
- 2 tsp. Coconut oil
- 4 cups Bone broth

Directions:

1. Warm the coconut oil in a pot and put in the garlic and ginger. Sauté for one minute before you put in the turmeric and curry powder and sautéing for one more minute.
2. Throw in celery, leeks, carrots, and cauliflower, continuously stirring for approximately one minute.
3. Put in the bone broth and chickpeas. Cover the pot and leave to boil. Reduce the heat and allow it to simmer for minimum fifteen minutes.
4. Turn off heat and put in parsley and kale, leaving the heat to cook the leaves.
5. Drizzle salt and pepper.
6. Serve.

Nutritional Info: Calories: 142 kcal || Protein: 8.64 g || Fat: 4.79 g || Carbohydrates: 17.57 g

---

GREEK SPLIT PEA SOUP

Time To Prepare: fifteen minutes

Time to Cook: 2 hours

Yield: Servings 6

Ingredients:

- 1 pinch dried marjoram
- 1 potato (diced)
- 1½ pounds ham bone
- 2 onions (cut)
- 2 quarts cold water
- 2-1/4 cups dried split peas
- 3 carrots, (chopped)
- 3 stalks celery (chopped)
- Ground black pepper
- Salt

Directions:

1. Simmer the peas in a pot for a couple of minutes and then soak for an hour.
2. Put in ham bone, onion, marjoram, and seasoning.
3. Boil for 1½hours.
4. Remove bone and meat. Put in the meat (diced) to the soup.
5. Put the rest of the vegetables and cook until soft.

Nutritional Info: Calories: 310 kcal **||** Carbohydrates: 58 g **||** Fat: 20 g **||** Protein: 2 g

---

GREEN BLAST SOUP

Time To Prepare: ten minutes

Time to Cook: twenty minutes

Yield: Servings 4

Ingredients:

- ¼ cup chopped cashews (not necessary)
- ¼ cup extra-virgin olive oil
- ¼ teaspoon freshly ground black pepper
- 1 bunch Swiss chard, crudely chopped
- 1 fennel bulb, trimmed and thinly cut
- 1 garlic clove, peeled

- 1 teaspoon salt
- 2 leeks, white parts only, thinly cut
- 2 tablespoons apple cider vinegar
- 3 cups vegetable broth
- 4 cups crudely chopped kale
- 4 cups crudely chopped mustard greens

Directions:

1. In a large pot, heat the oil on high heat.
2. Put in the leeks, fennel, and garlic and sauté until tender, for approximately five minutes.
3. Put in the Swiss chard, kale, and mustard greens and sauté until the greens wilt, two to three minutes.
4. Pour the broth then bring to its boiling point.
5. Reduce the heat to a simmer and cook until the vegetables are completely tender and soft about five minutes.
6. Mix in the vinegar, salt, pepper, and cashews (if using).
7. Use an immersion blender to purée the soup in the pot until the desired smoothness is achieved before you serve.

Nutritional Info: Calories: 238 || Total Fat: 14g || Total Carbohydrates: 22g || Sugar: 4g || Fiber: 6g || Protein: 9g || Sodium: 1294mg

GUT-HEALING BONE BROTH

Time To Prepare: fifteen minutes

Time to Cook: 8 to one day

Yield: Servings 4

Ingredients:

- 1 medium onion, chopped
- 1 tablespoon apple cider vinegar
- 2 bay leaves
- 2 celery stalks, chopped
- 2 pounds beef marrow bones
- 3 medium carrots, chopped

- 4 garlic cloves
- Filtered water, to cover

Directions:

1. In a 6-quart slow cooker, mix the bones, garlic, carrots, celery, onion, bay leaves, and vinegar. Cover with filtered water. Set the cooker on low and simmer for minimum 8 hours and up to one day.
2. Skim off and discard any foam that forms on the surface. Ladle the broth through a fine-mesh sieve or cheesecloth to strain out the solids. Pour into airtight glass containers. The broth can be placed in the fridge for maximum one week; just boil it again before use. To freeze, let the broth fully cool and then fill jars up to an inch below the top to allow for expansion, and keep for four to 5 months.

Nutritional Info: Calories: 40 || Total Fat: 0g || Saturated Fat: 0g || Cholesterol: 0mg || Carbohydrates: 5g || Fiber: 0g || Protein: 6g

---

HAMBURGER & TOMATO SOUP

Time To Prepare: ten minutes

Time to Cook: 4 hours

Yield: Servings 6

Ingredients:

- ½ cup beef broth
- ½ cup no-sugar added marinara sauce
- ½ cup shredded cheddar cheese
- 1 pound lean ground beef
- 1 yellow onion, chopped
- 2 cloves garlic, chopped
- Salt & pepper, to taste

Directions:

1. Put in all the ingredients to a slow cooker minus the shredded cheese and cook on high for 4 hours.
2. Mix in the cheese before you serve.

Nutritional Info: Calories: 209 || Carbohydrates: 5g || Fiber: 1g Net || Carbohydrates: 4g || Fat: 9g || Protein: 26g

---

HARVEST STEW

Time To Prepare: fifteen minutes

Time to Cook: 60 minutes

Yield: Servings 6

Ingredients:

- ¼ cup flour
- ½ cup cut carrots
- ½ cup diced celery
- ¾ cup diced onions
- 1 bay leaf
- 1 leek, cleaned and diced
- 1 potato, peeled and diced
- 1 pound stewing beef cubes
- 2 cups diced zucchini
- 2 tablespoons olive oil
- 2 tablespoons Worcestershire sauce
- 2 tomatoes, chopped
- 3 sprigs fresh thyme
- 3 turnips, diced
- 4 cups low-sodium beef broth
- 6 garlic cloves, peeled
- Salt and pepper, to taste

Directions:

1. Brown the beef cubes in olive oil. Dust the flour on the meat and stir to coat and spread.
2. Put in the onions, carrots, celery, leek, garlic, zucchini, potato, turnips, tomatoes, bay leaf, thyme sprigs, and beef broth. Put to its boiling point, then reduce the heat and simmer for 60 minutes.

3. Take away the bay leaf and thyme sprigs. Put in the Worcestershire sauce, salt, and pepper. Serve hot.

Nutritional Info: Calories: 254 || Fat: 9.5 g || Protein: 20 g || Sodium: 514 mg || Fiber: 3.5 g || Carbohydrates: 22 g

---

HEARTY ROOT VEGETABLE SOUP

Time To Prepare: five minutes

Time to Cook: ten minutes

Yield: Servings 4

Ingredients:

- 1 bay leaf
- 1 carrot, cut
- 1 celery, diced
- 1 garlic clove, minced
- 1 parsnip, cut
- 1 tablespoon fresh parsley, roughly chopped
- 1 teaspoon fresh sage
- 2 cups cauliflower, cut into little florets
- 4 cups chicken stock
- 4 tablespoons olive oil
- Kosher salt and freshly ground black pepper, to taste

Directions:

1. Simply drop all of the above ingredients into your Instant Pot.
2. Secure the lid. Choose "Manual" mode and High pressure; cook for about ten minutes. Once cooking is complete, use a natural pressure release; cautiously remove the lid.
3. Taste, calibrate the seasonings and serve instantly. Enjoy!

Nutritional Info: 190 Calories || 15.6g Fat || 6.1g Total Carbs || 6.7g Protein || 2.6g Sugars

---

HUNGARIAN LENTIL SOUP

Time To Prepare: fifteen minutes

Time to Cook: 2 hours

Yield: Servings 8

Ingredients:

- 7 Cups Chicken Stock
- 3 Carrots (Diced)
- 2 Stalks Celery (Diced)
- 1 Teaspoon Garlic (Minced)
- 2 Bay Leaves
- 1 Sprig Fresh Parsley (Chopped)
- 2 Tablespoons Olive Oil
- 2 Large Onions (Cubed)
- Salt
- Ground Black Pepper
- 1½ Cups Lentils (Soaked, Rinsed, Drained)
- ½ Teaspoon Paprika
- ½ Cup Grated Parmesan Cheese
- 3½ Cups Crushed Tomatoes
- 3/4 Cup White Wine

Directions:

1. Sauté onions in oil until shiny and put in garlic, paprika, celery, and carrots, cooking for about ten minutes.
2. Mix in tomatoes, chicken stock, lentils, bay leaves, seasoning, and wine to boil.
3. Cook until the lentils are soft.
4. Top with parsley and Parmesan before you serve.

Nutritional Info: Calories: 258 kcal **||** Carbohydrates: 34 g **||** Fat: 6 g **||** Protein: 14 g

---

ITALIAN BEEF SOUP

Time To Prepare: ten minutes

Time to Cook: 4 hours

Yield: Servings 6

Ingredients:

- ½ cup diced tomatoes
- ½ cup shredded mozzarella cheese
- 1 cup beef broth
- 1 cup heavy cream
- 1 pound lean ground beef
- 1 tablespoon Italian seasoning
- 1 yellow onion, chopped
- 2 cloves garlic, chopped
- Salt & pepper, to taste

Directions:

1. Put in all the ingredients to a slow cooker minus the heavy cream and mozzarella cheese. Cook on high for 4 hours.
2. Warm the heavy cream, and then put in the warmed cream and cheese to the soup. Stir thoroughly before you serve.

Nutritional Info: Calories: 241 || Carbohydrates: 4g || Fiber: 1g Net || Carbohydrates: 3g || Fat: 14g || Protein: 25g

---

ITALIAN MODENA SOUP

Time To Prepare: two minutes

Time to Cook: 8 minutes

Yield: Servings 4

Ingredients:

- ½ cup Parmigiano-Reggiano cheese, shaved
- ½ teaspoon crushed chili
- 1 cup water
- 1 onion, chopped
- 1 tablespoon Italian seasonings
- 16 ounces Cotechino di Modena, cut

- 2 cups tomatoes, purée
- 2 tablespoons olive oil
- 3 cups roasted vegetable broth
- Sea salt and ground black pepper, to taste

Directions:

1. Push the "Sauté" button to heat up your Instant Pot. Once hot, heat the oil and sauté the onions until soft and translucent.
2. Now, put in the sausage and cook an additional three minutes,
3. Mix in tomatoes, broth, water, sea salt, black pepper, crushed chili, and Italian seasonings.
4. Secure the lid. Choose "Manual" mode and High pressure; cook for five minutes. Once cooking is complete, use a quick pressure release; cautiously remove the lid.
5. Top with shaved Parmigiano-Reggiano cheese and serve warm

Nutritional Info: 340 Calories ‖ 27.9g Fat ‖ 5g Total Carbs ‖ 14.1g Protein ‖ 2.6g Sugars

---

ITALIAN SUMMER SQUASH SOUP

Time To Prepare: ten minutes

Time to Cook: fifteen minutes

Yield: Servings 4

Ingredients:

- ½ cup shredded carrot
- 1 cup shredded yellow squash
- 1 cup shredded zucchini
- 1 garlic clove, minced
- 1 small red onion, thinly cut
- 1 tablespoon finely chopped fresh chives
- 1 teaspoon salt
- 2 tablespoons finely chopped fresh basil
- 2 tablespoons pine nuts
- 3 cups vegetable broth
- 3 tablespoons extra-virgin olive oil

Directions:

1. In a large pot, heat the oil using high heat.
2. Put in the onion and garlic and sauté until tender, five to seven minutes.
3. Put in the zucchini, yellow squash, and carrot and sauté until tender, one to two minutes.
4. Pour the broth and salt then bring to its boiling point.
5. Reduce the heat and cook until the vegetables are soft, one to two minutes.
6. Mix in the basil and chives and serve, sprinkled with the pine nuts.

Nutritional Info: Calories: 172 || Total Fat: 15g || Total Carbohydrates: 6g || Sugar: 3g || Fiber: 2g || Protein: 5g || Sodium: 1170mg

---

KUMARA & CHICKPEA SOUP

Time To Prepare: twenty-five minutes

Time to Cook: thirty-five minutes

Yield: Servings 6

Ingredients:

- 1 bay leaf
- 1 onion (chopped)
- 1 teaspoon dried basil
- 1 tomato (chopped)
- ½ teaspoon dried thyme
- 1/4 teaspoon paprika
- 2 cloves garlic (minced)
- 2 cups kumara (peeled, chopped)
- 2 tablespoons olive oil
- 200g garbanzo beans
- 3 cups chicken broth
- Ground black pepper
- Mixed vegetables
- Salt

Directions:

1. Sauté onion, garlic, and sweet potatoes in oil for five minutes.
2. Put in broth, bay leaf, herbs, and seasoning.
3. Boil until soft.
4. Put in tomato, beans, and chickpeas, simmering some more before you serve.

Nutritional Info: Calories: 197 kcal ǁ Carbohydrates: 30 g ǁ Fat: 6 g ǁ Protein: 7.5 g

LAMB STEW

Time To Prepare: five minutes

Time to Cook: 8 hours

Yield: Servings 6

Ingredients:

- 1 lamb stock cube
- 1 onion, roughly chopped
- 2 pounds (907 g) boneless lamb, cut into cubes
- 2 tablespoons olive oil, plus more for greasing the frying pan
- 2 teaspoons dried rosemary
- 3 cups water
- 4 garlic cloves, finely chopped
- From the cupboard:
- Salt and freshly ground black pepper, to taste

Directions:

1. Position the lamb into a mildly greased nonstick frying pan, and cook using high heat for a couple of minutes or until browned.
2. Grease a slow cooker with olive oil, then put in the cooked lamb, stock cube, rosemary, onion, garlic, salt, black pepper, and 3 cups of water. Blend to blend well.
3. Place the slow cooker lid on and cook on LOW for eight hours.
4. Take away the cooked lamb stew from the slow cooker and serve warm.

Nutritional Info: calories: 252 ǁ total fat: 9.5g ǁ carbs: 4.9g ǁ protein: 34.9g

LAMB TACO SOUP

Time To Prepare: ten minutes

Time to Cook: 4-6 hours minutes

Yield: Servings 6

Ingredients:

- ½ teaspoon cayenne pepper
- 1 cup diced tomatoes
- 1 cup shredded cheddar cheese
- 1 green bell pepper, chopped
- 1 pound ground lamb
- 1 teaspoon ground coriander
- 1 teaspoon ground cumin
- 1 teaspoon paprika
- 1 yellow onion, chopped
- 2 cloves garlic, chopped
- 4 cups beef broth
- Salt & pepper, to taste

Directions:

1. Put in all the ingredients to a slow cooker minus the shredded cheese and cook on high for four to 6 hours.
2. Mix in the shredded cheese before you serve.

Nutritional Info: Calories: 265 ‖ Carbohydrates: 6g ‖ Fiber: 1g Net ‖ Carbohydrates: 5g ‖ Fat: 13g ‖ Protein: 30g

---

LEBANESE LENTIL SOUP

Time To Prepare: fifteen minutes

Time to Cook: 60 minutes

Yield: Servings 6

Ingredients:

- 1 cup brown lentils

- 1 lemon juiced
- 1 medium onion
- 1 tablespoon olive oil
- 2 medium carrots
- 2 teaspoons cinnamon
- 2 teaspoons cumin
- 3 stalks celery
- 4 cloves garlic
- 4 cups chicken broth low sodium
- 4 cups water
- 8 cups spinach
- salt& pepper to taste

Directions:

1. Over moderate heat, heat oil in a soup pot, Put in & cook carrots, celery & onions until become soft for seven minutes, put in pepper & salt to taste.
2. Stir cumin, cinnamon & garlic heat it for 30-60 minutes. Put in lentils & heat for a couple of minutes to slightly toast. Pour in the lemon juice, water & chicken broth, then bring the pot to its boiling point. When lentils are soft, decrease the heat to low & simmer, approximately 30-45 minutes.
3. Before you serve, mix in the spinach, cook until the color is green, now served to put in pepper, lemon juice & salt.

Nutritional Info: Calories: 102 kcal || Protein: 6.33 g || Fat: 4.58 g || Carbohydrates: 11.6 g

LEEK, CHICKEN AND SPINACH SOUP

Time To Prepare: ten minutes

Time to Cook: fifteen minutes

Yield: Servings 4

Ingredients:

- ¼ teaspoon freshly ground black pepper
- 1 tablespoon thinly cut fresh chives
- 1 teaspoon salt

- 2 cups shredded rotisserie chicken
- 2 leeks, white parts only, thinly cut
- 2 teaspoons grated or minced lemon zest
- 3 tablespoons unsalted butter
- 4 cups baby spinach
- 4 cups chicken broth

Directions:

1. In a large pot, melt the butter on high heat.
2. Put in the leeks and sauté until tender and starting to brown, three to five minutes.
3. Put in the spinach, broth, salt, and pepper and bring to its boiling point.
4. Reduce the heat and cook till the spinach wilts, one to two minutes.
5. Place the chicken and cook until warmed through one to two minutes.
6. Drizzle with the chives and lemon zest before you serve.

Nutritional Info: Calories: 256 || Total Fat: 12g || Total Carbohydrates: 9g || Sugar: 3g || Fiber: 2g || Protein: 27g || Sodium: 1483mg

---

LEMON CHICKEN SOUP

Time To Prepare: ten minutes

Time to Cook: 4 hours

Yield: Servings 4

Ingredients:

- ¼ cup freshly squeezed lemon juice
- 1 yellow onion, chopped
- 2 boneless, skinless chicken breasts
- 2 cloves garlic, chopped
- 2 tablespoons chives, chopped
- 6 cups chicken broth
- Salt & pepper, to taste

Directions:

1. Put in all the ingredients to a slow cooker and cook on high for 4 hours.

2. Once cooked, shred the chicken and stir back into the soup.

Nutritional Info: Calories: 171 || Carbohydrates: 6g || Fiber: 1g Net || Carbohydrates: 5g || Fat: 6g || Protein: 22g

---

MEDITERRANEAN STEW

Time To Prepare: ten minutes

Time to Cook: fifteen minutes

Yield: Servings 4

Ingredients:

- 1 (19-ounce) can cannellini beans, drained and washed
- 1 (fifteen½-ounce) can chickpeas, drained and washed
- 1 cup Basic Vegetable Stock or low-sodium canned vegetable stock
- 1 teaspoon dried oregano
- 1 teaspoon red pepper, crushed or to taste
- 1½ cups artichoke hearts, quartered
- 2 cups roasted tomatoes
- 3 cloves garlic, crushed and minced
- 3 tablespoons olive oil
- 4 tablespoons grated Parmesan cheese
- Chopped Italian parsley, for decoration
- Chopped sun-dried tomatoes, for decoration
- Crumbled feta cheese, for decoration
- Fresh oregano leaves, for decoration
- Freshly ground black pepper, to taste
- Garlic-seasoned croutons, for decoration
- Salt, to taste

Directions:

1. Warm the olive oil in a huge deep cooking pan on moderate heat and sauté the garlic for two to three minutes or until golden.
2. Lower the heat to moderate-low. Mix in the chickpeas, cannellini beans, roasted tomatoes, artichoke hearts, stock, Parmesan cheese, crushed red pepper, oregano, salt,

and pepper. Cook and stir for approximately ten minutes. Serve in separate bowls, garnishing as you wish.

Nutritional Info: Calories: 445 || Fat: 16 g || Protein: 18 g || Sodium: 530 mg || Fiber: 12 g || Carbohydrates: 61 g

---

MINESTRONE SOUP WITH QUINOA

Time To Prepare: ten minutes

Time to Cook: twenty minutes

Yield: Servings 6

Ingredients:

- ½ cup quinoa, washed well
- ½ red bell pepper, diced
- ½ teaspoon salt
- 1 (14 oz.) can cannellini beans, drained and washed well
- 1 (14 oz.) can diced tomatoes with its juice
- 1 bay leaf
- 1 cup packed kale, stemmed and meticulously washed
- 1 medium white onion, diced
- 1 small zucchini, diced
- 1 tablespoon freshly squeezed lemon juice
- 1 tablespoon ghee
- 2 carrots, chopped
- 2 celery stalks, diced
- 2 garlic cloves, minced
- 2 teaspoons dried rosemary
- 2 teaspoons dried thyme
- 5 cups vegetable broth
- Freshly ground black pepper

Directions:

1. In a huge soup pot on moderate heat, put in the ghee, garlic, onion, carrots, and celery, and sauté for about three minutes.
2. Put in the zucchini and red bell pepper, and sauté for a couple of minutes.
3. Mix in the broth, tomatoes, beans, kale, quinoa, lemon juice, rosemary, thyme, bay leaf, and salt, and flavor with black pepper. Put it to a simmer, reduce the heat temperature, cover, and cook for fifteen minutes, or until the quinoa is cooked. Take away the bay leaf and discard it. Serve hot.

Nutritional Info: Calories: 319 || Total Fat: 5g || Saturated Fat: 2g || Cholesterol: 0mg || Carbohydrates: 42g || Fiber: 9g || Protein: 18g

MOONG DAAL

Time To Prepare: fifteen minutes

Time to Cook: thirty minutes

Yield: Servings 6

Ingredients:

- ½ Cup Tomatoes (Diced)
- ½ Dried Red Chili Pepper
- ½ Teaspoon Ginger Root (Grated)
- ½ Teaspoon Ground Turmeric
- 1 Pinch Asafoetida
- 1 Teaspoon Cumin Seed
- 1 Teaspoon Jalapeno (Diced)
- 1/4 Cup Cilantro (Chopped)
- 2 Cloves Garlic (Chopped)
- 2 Teaspoons Vegetable Oil
- 2½ Cups Moong Dal (Rinsed)
- 2½ Cups Water
- 3 Teaspoons Lemon Juice
- Salt

Directions:

1. Soak daal for thirty minutes before boiling in water with salt until thick.

2. Put in ginger, jalapeno, tomato, lemon juice, and turmeric.
3. Heat cumin seed and red Chile pepper in a pan before you put in asafoetida powder and garlic.
4. Combine with split peas and serve with cilantro.

Nutritional Info: Calories: 330 kcal **||** Carbohydrates: 57 g **||** Fat: 3 g **||** Protein: 21 g

---

MUSHROOM AND THYME SOUP

Time To Prepare: five minutes

Time to Cook: twenty minutes

Yield: Servings 4

Ingredients:

- ¼ cup butter
- 12 ounces (340 g) wild mushrooms, chopped
- 2 garlic cloves, minced
- 2 teaspoons thyme leaves
- 4 cups vegetable broth
- 5 ounces (142 g) crème fraiche
- From the cupboard:
- Salt and freshly ground black pepper, to taste

Directions:

1. Place the butter in a deep cooking pan and melt on moderate heat.
2. Put in the minced garlic and cook for a minutes or until aromatic.
3. Put in the chopped mushrooms, and drizzle with salt and black pepper. Stir to blend and cook for about ten minutes or until the mushrooms are soft.
4. Put in the vegetable broth and bring the soup to its boiling point. Stir continuously. Reduce the heat and simmer the soup for about ten minutes or until it becomes slightly thick.
5. Pour the soup in a blender, and pulse until smooth, then fold in the crème fraiche.
6. Move the soup in a big container and top with thyme leaves before you serve.

Nutritional Info: calories: 282 **||** total fat: 25.1g **||** net carbs: 6.3g **||** protein: 7.8g

ONION, KALE AND WHITE BEAN SOUP

Time To Prepare: fifteen minutes

Time to Cook: twenty-five minutes

Yield: Servings 4

Ingredients:

- ⅛ Teaspoon red pepper flakes (not necessary)
- ¼ cup extra-virgin olive oil
- ¼ teaspoon freshly ground black pepper
- 1 (fifteen½-ounce) can white beans, drained and washed
- 1 big onion, thinly cut
- 1 teaspoon finely chopped fresh rosemary
- 1 teaspoon salt
- 2 garlic cloves, thinly cut
- 3 cups stemmed kale leaves cut into ½-inch pieces
- 4 cups vegetable broth

Directions:

1. In a large pot, heat the oil on high heat.
2. Lower the heat to moderate, and put in the onion, garlic, salt, pepper, and red pepper flakes (if using). Sauté until the onion is golden, approximately ten minutes.
3. Put in the kale, and sauté until wilted, one to two minutes.
4. Pour the broth then bring to its boiling point.
5. Lower the heat to simmer, and cook until the kale is tender about five minutes.
6. Put in the beans and rosemary. Cook until the beans are warmed through minimum two to three minutes before you serve.

Nutritional Info: Calories: 285 ‖ Total Fat: 15g ‖ Total Carbohydrates: 28g ‖ Sugar: 3g ‖ Fiber: 9g ‖ Protein: 13g ‖ Sodium: 1368mg

PORK STEW

Time To Prepare: five minutes

Time to Cook: 8 hours

Yield: Servings 6

Ingredients:

- 1 onion, finely chopped
- 1 teaspoon dried mixed spices (homemade or store-bought)
- 2 pounds (907 g) pork loin, cut into cubes
- 2 tablespoons olive oil
- 3 cups chicken stock
- 4 garlic cloves, crushed
- From the cupboard:
- Salt and freshly ground black pepper, to taste

Directions:

1. Grease the insert of the slow cooker with olive oil.
2. Combine the pork, chicken stock, onion, dried mixed spices, garlic, salt, and black pepper in the slow cooker.
3. Place the slow cooker lid on and cook on LOW for eight hours.
4. Ladle the stew in a big container and serve warm.

Nutritional Info: calories: 381 ‖ total fat: 18.3g ‖ carbs: 9.2g ‖ protein: 42.3g

---

PUMPKIN AND SAUSAGE SOUP

Time To Prepare: five minutes

Time to Cook: 33 minutes

Yield: Servings 4

Ingredients:

- ½ cup heavy whipping cream
- ½ cup pumpkin puree
- ½ teaspoon dried sage
- ½ teaspoon ground dried thyme
- ½ teaspoon red chili pepper flakes (not necessary)
- 1 garlic clove, minced
- 1 moderate-sized red onion, minced

- 1 pinch salt
- 1 small red bell pepper, diced
- 2 cups chicken broth
- 2 tablespoons butter, melted
- pounds (680 g) fresh sausage

Directions:

1. Sauté the sausage in a nonstick frying pan on moderate to high heat for a minutes, then put in the onion and bell pepper. Continue sautéing for about six minutes until the sausage is mildly browned and the onion is translucent.
2. Fold in the chili pepper flakes, thyme, sage, minced garlic, and salt, then put in the pumpkin puree, chicken broth, and heavy whipping cream.
3. Reduce the heat and bring them to a simmer using low heat for fifteen minutes or until it becomes thick.
4. Pour the cooked soup into a big serving container and put in the butter. Stir to mix thoroughly before you serve.

Nutritional Info: calories: 777 ‖ total fat: 70g ‖ net carbs: 7g ‖ fiber: 2g ‖ protein: 27g

---

PUMPKIN, COCONUT & SAGE SOUP

Time To Prepare: fifteen minutes

Time to Cook: thirty minutes

Yield: Servings 6

Ingredients:

- 1 cup canned pumpkin
- 1 cup full-fat coconut milk
- 1 teaspoon freshly chopped sage
- 2 cloves garlic, chopped
- 6 cups vegetable broth
- Pinch of salt & pepper, to taste

Directions:

1. Put in all the ingredients minus the coconut milk to a stockpot on moderate heat and bring to its boiling point. Reduce to a simmer and cook for half an hour
2. Put in the coconut milk and stir.

Nutritional Info: Calories: 146 || Carbohydrates: 7g || Fiber: 2g Net || Carbohydrates: 5g || Fat: 11g || Protein: 6g

---

QUICK MISO SOUP WITH WILTED GREENS

Time To Prepare: ten minutes

Time to Cook: five minutes

Yield: Servings 4

Ingredients:

- ½ teaspoon fish sauce
- 1 cup cut mushrooms
- 1 cup fresh baby spinach, meticulously washed
- 3 cups filtered water
- 3 cups vegetable broth
- 3 tablespoons miso paste
- 4 scallions, cut

Directions:

1. In a huge soup pot on high heat, put in the water, broth, mushrooms, and fish sauce, and bring to its boiling point. Turn off the heat.
2. In a small container, combine the miso paste with ½ cup of heated broth mixture to dissolve the miso. Mix the miso mixture back into the soup.
3. Mix in the spinach and scallions. Serve instantly.

Nutritional Info: Calories: 44 || Total Fat: 0 || Saturated Fat: 0g || Cholesterol: 0mg || Carbohydrates: 8g || Fiber: 1g || Protein: 2g

---

RED LENTIL DAL

Time To Prepare: ten minutes

Time to Cook: twenty minutes

Yield: Servings 6

Ingredients:

- ½ teaspoon salt
- 1 (14-ounce) can unsweetened coconut milk
- 1 bay leaf
- 1 cup red dried lentils, sorted and washed well
- 1 medium tomato, diced
- 1 medium white onion, diced
- 1 tablespoon coconut oil
- 1 teaspoon ground cumin
- 1 teaspoon ground ginger
- 1 teaspoon ground turmeric
- 1 teaspoon mustard seeds
- 1 teaspoon sesame seeds
- 2 garlic cloves, minced
- 2 tablespoons chopped fresh cilantro leaves
- 3 cups vegetable broth
- Dash ground cinnamon

Directions:

1. In a huge soup pot using high heat, combine the broth, lentils, and bay leaf, and place to its boiling point. Lessen the heat to moderate-low and simmer for about twenty minutes, or until the lentils are cooked.
2. In the meantime, in a moderate-sized deep cooking pan on moderate heat, sauté the onion and garlic in the coconut oil for a couple of minutes.
3. Put in the tomato, sesame seeds, ginger, cumin, turmeric, mustard seeds, salt, and cinnamon. Cook, regularly stirring, for five minutes.
4. Mix in the coconut milk, then put it to a simmer.
5. Remove and discard the bay leaf. Put in the coconut milk mixture to the lentils together with the cilantro, and stir until blended. Serve alone or over rice if you wish.

Nutritional Info: Calories: 283 || Total Fat: 6g || Saturated Fat: 5g || Cholesterol: 0mg || Carbohydrates: 32g || Fiber: 7g || Protein: 14g

RIBOLLITA

Time To Prepare: forty-five minutes

Time to Cook: 195 minutes

Yield: Servings 12

Ingredients:

- ½ Cup Olive Oil
- 1 Bunch Kale (Trimmed, Chopped)
- 1 Bunch Swiss Chard (Trimmed, Chopped)
- 1½ Cups Cabbage (Chopped)
- 12½ Inch-Thick Slices French Bread (Toasted)
- 2 Bay Leaves
- 2 Cups Dry Cannellini Beans (Rinsed)
- 2 Onions (Diced)
- 2 Potatoes (Peeled, Cut)
- 3 Carrots (Peeled, Sliced)
- 3 Large Stalks Celery (Chopped)
- 32 Ounce Chicken Broth
- 4 Cups Water
- 4 Sage Leaves
- 5 Cloves Garlic (Minced)
- Grated Parmesan Cheese
- Ground Black Pepper
- Ounce Tomatoes (Diced)
- Salt

Directions:

1. Boil beans in water for minimum five minutes and cool for 70 minutes.
2. Boil beans, garlic, sage leaves, bay leaves, and salt in chicken broth until soft.
3. Discard the leaves from half of the mixture.
4. Combine the remaining until the desired smoothness is achieved. Set aside.
5. Cook onions in oil, putting in carrots, potatoes, cabbage, celery, Swiss chard, and kale, tomatoes, and seasoning for about twenty minutes.

6. Put in the pureed bean and cook for forty minutes before you put in the rest of the mixture.
7. Put in toasted bread slices. Heat the soup for about twenty minutes.
8. Serve with Parmesan cheese and olive oil.

Nutritional Info: Calories: 418 kcal || Carbohydrates: 41.8 g || Fat: 22 g || Protein: 14 g

RICH ONION AND BEEF STEW

Time To Prepare: five minutes

Time to Cook: 10 hours

Yield: Servings 6

Ingredients:

- 1 beef stock cube
- 1 teaspoon dried mixed herbs (such as Italian seasoning)
- 2 onions, roughly chopped
- 2 pounds (907 g) boneless stewing beef, cut into cubes
- 3 cups water
- 3 tablespoons olive oil, divided
- 5 garlic cloves, crushed
- From the cupboard:
- Salt and freshly ground black pepper, to taste

Directions:

1. Grease the insert of the slow cooker with 2 tablespoons of olive oil. Coat a nonstick frying pan with the rest of the olive oil.
2. Heat the oil in the frying pan on moderate to high heat, then put the beef in the frying pan and sear for a couple of minutes or until medium-rare. Shake the frying pan continuously to sear the beef cubes uniformly.
3. Position the cooked beef in the slow cooker, then put in the stock cube, mixed herbs, garlic, onions, salt, black pepper, and water. Stir to mix thoroughly.
4. Place the slow cooker lid on and cook on LOW for ten hours.
5. Ladle the stew in a big container and serve warm.

Nutritional Info: calories: 199 || total fat: 6.3g || carbs: 1.9g || protein: 33.8g

---

ROASTED BUTTERNUT SQUASH APPLE SOUP

Time To Prepare: ten minutes

Time to Cook: forty minutes

Yield: Servings 4

Ingredients:

- 1 butternut squash
- 1 celery rib
- 1 cup water
- 1 small onion
- 1/4 teaspoon cinnamon
- 1/4 teaspoon ginger
- 1/4 teaspoon nutmeg
- 2 red, sweet apples
- 3 cups low-sodium chicken/vegetable stock
- 4 tablespoons olive oil
- Salt & pepper to taste

Directions:

1. Preheat your oven to 400°F.
2. Put diced apple on a one-sheet pan & put the diced butternut squash on the second sheet pan.
3. Allow season to squash olive oil & put in pepper & salt. Stir get everything mix thoroughly. Put in apple with one tablespoon olive oil & stir to coat.
4. Apple & Roast squash for around half an hour, until browned.
5. Heat olive oil (remaining 1 ½ tablespoons) in a big stockpot.
6. Sauté celery & onion for around seven minutes, until soft. Put in Pepper & salt to taste.
7. Put in vegetable or chicken stock & water & bring to a simmer.
8. Once the apple & squash are roasted, put in them to the pot. Put in cinnamon, nutmeg & ginger.

9. Now blend the soup until the desired smoothness is achieved. Season pepper & salt to taste.
10. Serve with desired toppings.

Nutritional Info: Calories: 251 kcal ‖ Protein: 4.06 g ‖ Fat: 15.93 g ‖ Carbohydrates: 25.14 g

RUSSIAN CABBAGE SOUP (SHCHI)

Time To Prepare: ten minutes

Time to Cook: twenty minutes

Yield: Servings 6

Ingredients:

- ½ big head cabbage, shredded
- ½ teaspoon salt
- 1 (14 oz.) can diced tomatoes with its juice
- 1 bay leaf
- 1 big potato, peeled and diced
- 1 celery stalk, diced
- 1 medium white onion, diced
- 1 tablespoon ghee
- 2 carrots, shredded
- 3 garlic cloves, minced
- 6 cups vegetable broth
- Freshly ground black pepper

Directions:

1. In a huge soup pot using high heat, mix the broth, bay leaf, and potato, and bring to its boiling point. Lower the heat to low and simmer for fifteen minutes.
2. In the meantime, in a moderate-sized deep cooking pan on moderate heat, heat the ghee. Place the onion and garlic, and sauté for five minutes.
3. Put in the carrots, celery, and cabbage, and cook for a couple of minutes, stirring frequently. Move to the soup pot.

4. Mix in the tomatoes and salt, and flavor with pepper. Mix thoroughly and carry on simmering until all ingredients have become tender and cooked, approximately five minutes. Take off and discard the bay leaf, and serve instantly.

Nutritional Info: Calories: 180 || Total Fat: 3g || Saturated Fat: 2g || Cholesterol: 7mg || Carbohydrates: 20g || Fiber: 5g || Protein: 12g

---

SAFFRON AND SALMON SOUP

Time To Prepare: ten minutes

Time to Cook: twenty minutes

Yield: Servings 4

Ingredients:

- ¼ cup extra-virgin olive oil
- ¼ tsp. freshly ground black pepper
- ¼ tsp. saffron threads
- ½ cup dry white wine
- 1 lb. salmon fillets, cut into 1-inch pieces
- 1 tsp. salt
- 2 cups baby spinach
- 2 garlic cloves, thinly cut
- 2 leeks, white parts only, thinly cut
- 2 medium carrots, thinly cut
- 2 tablespoons chopped scallions, both white and green parts
- 2 tablespoons finely chopped fresh flat-leaf parsley
- 4 cups vegetable broth

Directions:

1. In a large pot, heat the oil using high heat.
2. Put in the leeks, carrots, and garlic and sauté until tender, five to seven minutes.
3. Pour the broth then bring to its boiling point.
4. Reduce the heat to a simmer then put in the salmon, salt, pepper, and saffron. Cook until the salmon is thoroughly cooked, minimum 8 minutes.

5. Put in the spinach, wine, scallions, and parsley and cook until the spinach has wilted, one to two minutes, before you serve.

Nutritional Info: Calories: 418 || Total Fat: 26g || Total Carbohydrates: 13g || Sugar: 4g || Fiber: 2g || Protein: 29g || Sodium: 1455mg

SLOW COOKER LAMB & CAULIFLOWER SOUP

Time To Prepare: ten minutes

Time to Cook: 4 hours

Yield: Servings 6

Ingredients:

- ½ teaspoon cracked black pepper
- ½ teaspoon salt
- 1 cauliflower head, cut into florets
- 1 cup heavy cream
- 1 pound ground lamb
- 1 tablespoon freshly chopped thyme
- 1 yellow onion, chopped
- 2 cloves garlic, chopped
- 5 cups beef broth

Directions:

1. Put in the ground lamb and cauliflower to the base of a stockpot.
2. Put in in the rest of the ingredients minus the heavy cream, and cook on high for 4 hours.
3. Warm the heavy cream before you put in to the soup. Use an immersion blender to combine the soup until creamy.

Nutritional Info: Calories: 263 || Carbohydrates: 6g || Fiber: 2g Net || Carbohydrates: 4g || Fat: 14g || Protein: 27g

SPICY ASIAN-STYLE SOUP

Time To Prepare: ten minutes

Yield: Servings 4

Ingredients:

- ½ cup soy milk
- ½ pound asparagus, diced
- 1 bay leaf
- 1 cup celery, diced
- 1 shallot, diced
- 1 tablespoon coconut aminos
- 1 teaspoon Taco seasoning
- 1/4 teaspoon freshly ground black pepper
- 2 chicken bouillon cubes
- 2 cloves garlic, diced
- 2 cups Crimini mushrooms
- 2 tablespoons butter, softened
- 4 cups water
- Sea salt and black pepper, to taste

Directions:

1. Push the "Sauté" button to heat up your Instant Pot. Once hot, melt the butter; then, sweat the shallot until tender.
2. Mix in garlic; cook an additional 40 seconds, stirring regularly.
3. Put in the rest of the ingredients.
4. Secure the lid. Choose "Manual" mode and High pressure; cook for seven minutes. Once cooking is complete, use a quick pressure release; cautiously remove the lid.
5. Ladle into separate bowls and serve warm. Enjoy!

Nutritional Info: 104 Calories || 7g Fat || 6.6g Total Carbs || 3.9g Protein || 3.5g Sugars

---

SPICY CABBAGE TURMERIC COCONUT SOUP

Time To Prepare: ten minutes

Time to Cook: twenty minutes

Yield: Servings 4

Ingredients:

- ½ teaspoon black pepper
- ½ teaspoon salt
- 1 head white cabbage
- 1 teaspoon cumin powder
- 1/4 cup coconut milk
- 2 cloves garlic
- 2 tablespoons coconut oil
- 2 teaspoons turmeric powder
- 3 cups vegetable/chicken stock

Directions:

1. Heat the oil in a frying pan on moderate heat.
2. Put in the cabbage & garlic & sauté until the cabbage is delicate.
3. Put in the stock, bubble, spread, & stew for about twenty minutes.
4. Turn off the heat, including the coconut milk & flavors.
5. Blend until the desired smoothness is achieved & season to taste. Serve, gulp & appreciate!

Nutritional Info: Calories: 207 kcal ‖ Protein: 13.52 g ‖ Fat: 10.79 g ‖ Carbohydrates: 16.84 g

---

SPICY LIME-CHICKEN "TORTILLA-LESS" SOUP

Time To Prepare: ten minutes

Time to Cook: twenty minutes

Yield: Servings 6

Ingredients:

- ¼ teaspoon cayenne pepper
- ½ teaspoon salt
- 1 (14 oz.) can diced tomatoes, and it's juice
- 1 (4oz.) can diced green chiles
- 1 avocado, cut
- 1 jalapeño pepper, seeded and minced

- 1 medium white onion, diced
- 1 pound shredded cooked chicken
- 1 tablespoon avocado oil
- 1 teaspoon chili powder
- 1 teaspoon ground cumin
- 3 garlic cloves, minced
- 3 tablespoons freshly squeezed lime juice
- 6 cups chicken broth or vegetable broth
- Fresh cilantro, for decoration
- Freshly ground black pepper

Directions:

1. In a huge soup pot on moderate heat, heat the avocado oil.
2. Put in the garlic, onion, and jalapeño pepper, and sauté for five minutes.
3. Mix in the broth, chicken, tomatoes, green chiles, lime juice, chili powder, cumin, salt, and cayenne pepper, and flavor with black pepper. Put it to a simmer, and cook for about ten minutes.
4. Serve hot, topped with slices of avocado and decorated with cilantro.

Nutritional Info: Calories: 283 || Total Fat: 7g || Saturated Fat: 1g || Cholesterol: 47mg || Carbohydrates: 12g || Fiber: 3g || Protein: 29g

---

SPICY RAMEN NOODLES

Time To Prepare: fifteen minutes

Time to Cook: 0 minutes

Yield: Servings 4

Ingredients:

- ¼ cup chopped fresh cilantro
- ¼ cup cut scallion
- ¼ cup thinly cut cucumber
- 1 tablespoon coconut aminos
- 1 tablespoon freshly squeezed lime juice
- 1 tablespoon grated peeled fresh ginger

- 1 tablespoon raw honey
- 1 teaspoon chili powder
- 2 tablespoons rice vinegar
- 2 tablespoons sesame oil
- 2 tablespoons sesame seeds
- 8 ounces buckwheat noodles or rice noodles, cooked

Directions:

1. In a big serving container, meticulously mix the noodles, sesame seeds, cucumber, scallion, cilantro, sesame oil, vinegar, ginger, coconut aminos, honey, lime juice, and chili powder.
2. Split among 4 soup bowls and serve at room temperature.

Nutritional Info: Calories: 663 || Total Fat: 28g || Saturated Fat: 4g || Cholesterol: 0mg || Carbohydrates: 115g || Fiber: 39g || Protein: 21g

---

SPICY SEAFOOD STEW

Time To Prepare: ten minutes

Time to Cook: twenty minutes

Yield: Servings 6

Ingredients:

- ¼ cup freshly squeezed lime juice
- ½ cup chopped fresh cilantro
- ½ cup chopped yellow onion
- ½ cup coconut milk
- ½ cup diced green pepper
- ½ cup thinly cut scallions
- ¾ pound medium-size shrimp, shelled and deveined
- ¾ pound skinless firm-fleshed fish fillets, (cod, center-cut salmon, or halibut)
- 1 tablespoon minced garlic
- 1 teaspoon hot pepper sauce
- 2 tablespoons olive oil

- 3 cups canned peeled, chopped tomatoes, undrained
- Seasoned salt, to taste

Directions:

1. Warm the oil in a huge nonstick frying pan on moderate to high heat. Put in the onions, green pepper, garlic, and tomatoes. Put to a simmer while stirring once in a while, then cook for three to four minutes.
2. Put in the coconut milk, pepper sauce, lime juice, and seasoned salt. Set to a simmer and cook for minimum 2 minutes. Put in the fish and stir, being cautious not to break apart the fillets. Cook till the fish is thoroughly cooked, approximately eight minutes. Put in the shrimp and cook until opaque and thoroughly cooked, approximately five minutes.
3. To serve, use a slotted spoon to take equal amounts of the fish and shrimp to 4 shallow serving bowls. Place the sauce over the seafood and decorate with scallions and cilantro. Serve hot.

Nutritional Info: Calories: 219 ‖ Fat: 11 g ‖ Protein: 19g ‖ Sodium: 375 mg ‖ Fiber: 2 g ‖ Carbohydrates: 10 g

---

SWEET POTATO AND BLACK BEAN CHILI

Time To Prepare: ten minutes

Time to Cook: twenty minutes

Yield: Servings 8

Ingredients:

- ¼ teaspoon cayenne pepper
- ¼ teaspoon dried oregano
- ½ teaspoon ground cinnamon
- 1 (28-ounce) can diced tomatoes with their juice
- 1 green bell pepper, diced
- 1 red bell pepper, diced
- 1 red onion, diced
- 1 tablespoon chili powder
- 1 tablespoon freshly squeezed lime juice
- 1 teaspoon cocoa powder

- 1 teaspoon ground cumin
- 1 teaspoon salt
- 2 cups vegetable broth
- 2 tablespoons avocado oil
- 3 cups black beans, drained and washed well
- 3 cups cooked sweet potato cubes
- 5 garlic cloves, minced

Directions:

1. In a huge soup pot on moderate heat, warm the avocado oil.
2. Place the onion and garlic, and sauté for a couple of minutes.
3. Mix in the red bell pepper and the green bell pepper, and sauté for approximately 3 minutes until tender.
4. Put in the sweet potato, beans, broth, tomatoes, lime juice, chili powder, cocoa powder, cumin, salt, cinnamon, cayenne pepper, and oregano, then stir until blended. Put to a simmer, and cook for fifteen minutes. Serve instantly.

Nutritional Info: Calories: 160 ‖ Total Fat: 4g ‖ Saturated Fat: 0g ‖ Cholesterol: 0mg ‖ Carbohydrates: 29g ‖ Fiber: 6g ‖ Protein: 8g

---

SWEET POTATO AND CORN SOUP

Time To Prepare: ten minutes

Time to Cook: twenty minutes

Yield: Servings 4

Ingredients:

- ¼ cup extra-virgin olive oil or coconut oil
- ¼ teaspoon freshly ground black pepper
- 1 cup broccoli florets
- 1 cup coconut milk or almond milk
- 1 cup frozen corn kernels
- 1 cup thinly cut mushrooms
- 1 medium zucchini, cut into ¼-inch dice
- 1 small onion, cut into ¼-inch dice

- 1 teaspoon salt
- 2 cups peeled sweet potatoes cut into ¼-inch dice
- 2 tablespoons finely chopped fresh flat-leaf parsley
- 4 cups vegetable broth

Directions:

1. In a large pot, heat the oil on high heat.
2. Put in the zucchini, broccoli, mushrooms, and onion and sauté until tender, 5 to 8 minutes.
3. Pour the broth and sweet potatoes and place it to its boiling point.
4. Lower the heat to a simmer and cook until the sweet potatoes are soft, five to seven minutes.
5. Put in the corn, coconut milk, parsley, salt, and pepper. Cook on low heat up to the corn is thoroughly heated before you serve.

Nutritional Info: Calories: 402 || Total Fat: 29g || Total Carbohydrates: 31g || Sugar: 9g || Fiber: 6g || Protein: 10g || Sodium: 1406mg

---

TEX-MEX CHICKEN SOUP

Time To Prepare: ten minutes

Time to Cook: 1 hour

Yield: Servings 4

Ingredients:

- ¼ cup roasted pumpkin seeds
- 1 teaspoon paprika powder
- 1 yellow onion, chopped
- 1¾ cups coconut cream
- 12 ounces (340 g) boneless chicken thighs
- 2 tablespoons coconut oil
- 3 tablespoons Tex-Mex seasoning
- 4 tablespoons lime juice
- Fresh cilantro, chopped
- Salt and ground black pepper, to taste

Directions:

1. Cook the chicken thighs in a pot of water, covered, for thirty minutes or until the chicken is completely fork-soft. Move the chicken to a container and reserve the chicken broth until ready to use.
2. Warm the coconut oil in a nonstick frying pan on moderate heat, then put in the onion and drizzle with Tex-Mex seasoning, salt, and pepper. sauté for five minutes until the onion is translucent.
3. Pour over the reserved chicken broth and coconut cream. Bring them to a simmer for about twenty minutes or until it becomes thick.
4. Put in the chicken, pumpkin seeds, paprika powder, lime juice, and cilantro to the soup. Stir to blend well before you serve.

Nutritional Info: calories: 730 ‖ total fat: 63g ‖ net carbs: 19g ‖ fiber: 9g ‖ protein: 23g

THAI CHICKEN NOODLE SOUP

Time To Prepare: ten minutes

Time to Cook: ten minutes

Yield: Servings 2-3

Ingredients:

- 6 cups low-sodium chicken broth
- 1 stalk lemongrass, minced
- 1 bay leaf
- 1 tablespoon ginger, grated
- 1 big carrot, cut
- 1 cup broccoli florets, trimmed
- 1 cup mushrooms, quartered
- ½ teaspoon. cayenne pepper
- 3 cloves garlic, minced
- 2 Tablespoon. gluten-free soy sauce
- Salt and black pepper (to taste)
- a handful of fresh cilantro, chopped
- 1-2 fresh chicken breasts, chopped

- 1/4 cup fresh lime juice
- 1/4 cup coconut milk
- 8-10 oz. gluten-free flat Thai rice noodles

Directions:

1. Boil noodles in accordance with package directions, or until firm to the bite. Drain and save for later.
2. Pour chicken broth in a big pot and bring to its boiling point using high heat. Put in chicken, broccoli, mushrooms, lemongrass, ginger, carrot, bay leaf. Turn heat to high and let the broth boil for a minute. Cover the pot and decrease the heat to moderate. Simmer the soup for 6 more minutes.
3. While the soup is simmering, mix in cayenne, garlic, lime juice, and soy sauce. Turn heat to low and put in the coconut milk; stir thoroughly.
4. Put cooked noodles into bowls. Pour soup over the noodles, then drizzle with cilantro.

Nutritional Info: Calories: 503 kcal **||** Protein: 48.11 g **||** Fat: 19.63 g **||** Carbohydrates: 35.9 g

---

THAI WINTER VEGETABLE SOUP

Time To Prepare: 60 minutes

Time to Cook: 6 hours

Yield: Servings 12

Ingredients:

- ½ Of Lemon Juice
- 1 Lime Juice
- 1 Piece Ginger (Peeled, Grated)
- 1 Teaspoon Cumin
- 14 Ounce Coconut Milk
- 14 Ounce Peeled Italian Plum Tomatoes
- 2 Large Onions (Peeled, Quartered)
- 2 Stalks Lemongrass (Split)
- 3 Carrots (Peeled, Chopped)
- 3 Cloves Garlic (Peeled, Chopped)
- 3 Red Bell Peppers (Quartered, Seeded)

- 4 Large Sweet Potatoes (Peeled, Cut)
- 4 Tablespoons Cilantro (Chopped)
- Ground Black Pepper
- Optional: 1 Green Chili Pepper (Chopped)
- Salt

Directions:

1. Cook the vegetables with ginger and chili before pouring in coconut milk.
2. Mix in cilantro, cumin, lemon juice, and seasoning, cooking for around six hours.
3. Remove lemongrass and blend until thick.
4. Put in lime juice, seasoning, and cilantro to serve.

Nutritional Info: Calories: 468 kcal ‖ Carbohydrates: 81 g ‖ Fat: fifteen g ‖ Protein: 8.5 g

TOMATO AND BASIL SOUP

Time To Prepare: five minutes

Time to Cook: fifteen minutes

Yield: Servings 4

Ingredients:

- ¼ cup chopped fresh basil leaves
- ¼ cup heavy whipping cream
- 1 (14.5-ounce / 411-g) can diced tomatoes
- 2 ounces (57 g) cream cheese
- 4 tablespoons butter
- From the cupboard:
- Salt and freshly ground black pepper, to taste

Directions:

1. Position the diced tomatoes in a food processor. Process until the desired smoothness is achieved.
2. Melt the butter in a deep cooking pan on moderate heat. Put in the tomato purée, cream, and cheese. Cook for about ten minutes or until well blended. Keep stirring during the cooking.

3. Drizzle with chopped basil leaves, salt, and black pepper. Keep cooking for another five minutes or until the desired smoothness is achieved and the soup has become thick. Stir continuously.
4. Ladle the soup into a big container and serve warm.

Nutritional Info: calories: 238 || total fat: 22.1g || total carbs: 8.9g || fiber: 2.1g || net carbs: 6.8g || protein: 3.1g

---

TOMATO BISQUE SOUP

Time To Prepare: ten minutes

Time to Cook: forty minutes

Yield: Servings 6

Ingredients:

- 1 cup heavy cream
- 1 teaspoon freshly chopped thyme
- 2 tablespoons butter
- 3 cloves garlic, chopped
- 3 cups canned whole, peeled tomatoes
- 4 cups chicken broth
- Salt & black pepper, to taste

Directions:

1. Put in the butter to the bottom of a stockpot.
2. Put in in all the rest of the ingredients minus the heavy cream. Bring to its boiling point, and then simmer for forty minutes.
3. Warm the heavy cream, and then mix into the soup.

Nutritional Info: Calories: 144 || Carbohydrates: 4g || Fiber: 1g Net || Carbohydrates: 3g || Fat: 12g || Protein: 4g

---

TURKEY MEATBALL SOUP

Time To Prepare: fifteen minutes

Time to Cook: fifteen minutes

Yield: Servings 6

Ingredients:

For the Meatballs:

- ¼ teaspoon red pepper flakes
- ½ teaspoon dried oregano
- ½ teaspoon salt
- 1 pound ground turkey
- 1 tablespoon Dijon mustard
- 1 tablespoon ghee
- 1 teaspoon dried basil
- 1 teaspoon garlic powder
- Freshly ground black pepper

For the Soup:

- ½ teaspoon dried thyme
- 1 bay leaf
- 1 medium white onion, diced
- 2 carrots, diced
- 2 cups shredded kale leaves, stemmed and meticulously washed
- 2 garlic cloves, minced
- 6 cups vegetable broth

Directions:

To make the Meatballs:

1. In a moderate-sized container, put the turkey, mustard, basil, garlic powder, oregano, salt, and red pepper flakes, and flavor with pepper. With your hands, combine the ingredients until they are well blended.
2. Put in the ghee to a stockpot on moderate to high heat. Roll the meat mixture into 1-inch balls and layer across the bottom of the pot. Cook for minimum 2 minutes per side, until almost thoroughly cooked. Move the meatballs to a plate.

To make the Soup:

1. To the stockpot, put in the onion, carrots, garlic, and thyme. Cook for approximately 2 minutes, slowly stirring, until the onions are translucent.
2. Put in the broth, kale, bay leaf, and meatballs. Put to a simmer, lessen the heat to moderate-low and simmer for approximately fifteen minutes until the meatballs are thoroughly cooked, and the kale has tenderized. Remove and discard the bay leaf. Serve hot.

Nutritional Info: Calories: 259 || Total Fat: 14g || Saturated Fat: 5g || Cholesterol: 88mg || Carbohydrates: 9g || Fiber: 2g || Protein: 26g

TUSCAN STYLE SOUP

Time To Prepare: three minutes

Time to Cook: five minutes

Yield: Servings 4

Ingredients:

- ½ cup leeks, cut
- 1 carrot, trimmed and grated
- 1 zucchini, shredded
- 1/4 teaspoon ground black pepper
- 2 cups broth, if possible homemade
- 2 cups water
- 2 garlic cloves, minced
- 2 tablespoons butter, melted
- 4 cups broccoli rabe, broken into pieces
- Sea salt, to taste

Directions:

1. Push the "Sauté" button to heat up your Instant Pot; now, melt the butter. Cook the leeks for approximately 2 minutes or until tender.
2. Put in minced garlic and cook an additional 40 seconds.
3. Put in the rest of the ingredients. Secure the lid.
4. "Manual" mode and Low pressure; cook for about three minutes. Once cooking is complete, use a quick pressure release; cautiously remove the lid. Enjoy!

Nutritional Info: 95 Calories || 6.7g Fat || 5.2g Total Carbs || 4.2g Protein || 1.4g Sugars

---

VEGETABLE BEEF SOUP

Time To Prepare: ten minutes

Time to Cook: 4-6 hours

Yield: Servings 6

Ingredients:

- ½ cup diced tomatoes
- 1 pound lean ground beef
- 1 teaspoon freshly chopped rosemary
- 1 teaspoon freshly chopped thyme
- 1 yellow onion, chopped
- 1 zucchini, diced
- 2 cloves garlic, chopped
- 2 stalks celery, chopped
- 4 cups beef broth
- Salt & pepper, to taste

Directions:

1. Put in all the ingredients to a slow cooker and cook on high for four to 6 hours.
2. Stir thoroughly before you serve.

Nutritional Info: Calories: 185 || Carbohydrates: 5g || Fiber: 1g Net || Carbohydrates: 4g || Fat: 6g || Protein: 7g

---

VEGETARIAN GARLIC, TOMATO & ONION SOUP

Time To Prepare: fifteen minutes

Time to Cook: thirty minutes

Yield: Servings 6

Ingredients:

- ½ cup full-fat unsweetened coconut milk
- 1 bay leaf
- 1 teaspoon Italian seasoning
- 1 yellow onion, chopped
- 1½ cups canned diced tomatoes
- 3 cloves garlic, chopped
- 6 cups vegetable broth
- Fresh basil, for serving
- Pinch of salt & pepper, to taste

Directions:

1. Put in all the ingredients minus the coconut milk and fresh basil to a stockpot on moderate heat and bring to its boiling point. Reduce to a simmer and cook for half an hour
2. Take away the bay leaf, and then use an immersion blender to combine the soup until the desired smoothness is achieved. Mix in the coconut milk.
3. Decorate using fresh basil before you serve.

Nutritional Info: Calories: 104 || Carbohydrates: 6g || Fiber: 1g Net || Carbohydrates: 5g || Fat: 7g || Protein: 6g

WEDDING SOUP

Time To Prepare: fifteen minutes

Time to Cook: 60 minutes

Yield: Servings 6

Ingredients:

- ¼ bunch fresh parsley, chopped
- ¾ pound lean ground beef
- 1 cup rough chopped fresh spinach with stems removed
- 1 egg or ¼ cup egg substitute
- 1 yellow onion, chopped
- 2 quarts Rich Poultry Stock or low-sodium canned chicken stock
- 2 sprigs fresh basil, chopped

- 3 cloves garlic, minced
- 3 slices Italian bread, toasted
- 3 sprigs fresh oregano, chopped
- 4 ounces fresh grated Parmesan cheese
- Freshly cracked black pepper, to taste

Directions:

1. Preheat your oven to 375°F.
2. Wet the toasted Italian bread with water, then squeeze out all the liquid.
3. In a big container, combine the bread, beef, egg, onion, garlic, parsley, oregano, basil, pepper, and half of the Parmesan. Form the mixture into 1- to two-inch balls; put in a baking dish and cook for twenty minutes to half an hour. Take off from the oven and drain using paper towels.
4. Steam the spinach firm to the bite. In a big stockpot, mix the stock, spinach, and meatballs; simmer for half an hour
5. Ladle the soup into serving bowls then top with the rest of the cheese

Nutritional Info: Calories: 245 ǁ Fat: 10 g ǁ Protein: 26 g ǁ Sodium: 1,021 mg ǁ Fiber: 0.5 g ǁ Carbohydrates: 9 g

---

WHITE VELVET CAULIFLOWER SOUP

Time To Prepare: ten minutes

Time to Cook: twenty minutes

Yield: Servings 6

Ingredients:

- 1 head cauliflower, chopped into 1-inch pieces
- 1 small celery root, peeled, cut into 1-inch pieces
- 1 small white onion, diced
- 1 tbsp. avocado oil
- 2 scallions, cut
- 2 tbsp. ghee
- 3 garlic cloves, minced
- 4 cups vegetable broth

Directions:

1. In a huge soup pot on moderate heat, heat the avocado oil.
2. Place the onion and garlic, and sauté for five minutes.
3. Place the celery root and cauliflower.
4. Raise the heat to moderate-high, then continue to sauté for minimum five minutes, or until the cauliflower starts to brown and caramelize the sides.
5. Mix in the broth and ghee and place it to its boiling point. Lessen the heat to moderate-low and simmer for about ten minutes. Take away the pot from the heat.
6. Use an immersion blender to or in batches in a standard blender, purée the soup until creamy. Serve instantly, sprinkled with the scallions.

Nutritional Info: Calories: 183 || Total Fat: 8g || Saturated Fat: 3g || Cholesterol: 0mg || Carbohydrates: 10g || Fiber: 3g || Protein: 9g

---

WHOLESOME CABBAGE SOUP

Time To Prepare: two minutes

Time to Cook: 8 minutes

Yield: Servings 4

Ingredients:

- ½ pound Capocollo, chopped
- ½ teaspoon cayenne pepper
- 1 bay leaf
- 1 celery stalk, chopped
- 1 cup tomatoes, puréed
- 1 cup water
- 1 onion, chopped
- 1 parsnip, chopped
- 1 pound cabbage, cut into wedges
- 2 cups broth, if possible homemade
- Coarse sea salt and ground black pepper, to your preference

Directions:

1. Put in all of the above ingredients to your Instant Pot.
2. Secure the lid. Choose "Manual" mode and High pressure; cook for about three minutes. Once cooking is complete, use a quick pressure release; cautiously remove the lid.
3. Ladle into four soup bowls and serve hot. Enjoy!

Nutritional Info: 258 Calories || 20.4g Fat || 6g Total Carbs || 9.9g Protein || 3.6g Sugars

---

ZESTY BROCCOLI SOUP

Time To Prepare: ten minutes

Time to Cook: twenty minutes

Yield: Servings 4

Ingredients:

- ½ teaspoon freshly squeezed lemon juice
- ½ teaspoon lemon zest
- ½ teaspoon salt
- 1 carrot, chopped
- 1 celery stalk, diced
- 1 head broccoli, roughly chopped
- 1 medium white onion, diced
- 1 tablespoon ghee
- 3 cups vegetable broth
- 3 garlic cloves, minced
- Freshly ground black pepper

Directions:

1. In a huge soup pot on moderate heat, melt the ghee.
2. Place the onion and garlic, and sauté for five minutes.
3. Put in the broccoli, carrot, and celery, and sauté for a couple of minutes.
4. Mix in the broth, salt, lemon juice, and lemon zest, and flavor with pepper. Heat to a simmer, and cook for minimum ten minutes. Serve instantly.

Nutritional Info: Calories: 80 || Total Fat: 4g || Saturated Fat: 2g || Cholesterol: 0mg || Carbohydrates: 10g || Fiber: 3g || Protein: 2g

ZUCCHINI AND CHICKEN BROTH

Time To Prepare: twenty minutes

Time to Cook: twenty minutes

Yield: Servings 2

Ingredients:

- ¾ cup coconut milk
- 1 big zucchini, thinly cut
- 1 pound (454 g) boneless, skinless chicken breasts, cut into little pieces
- 1 tablespoon fresh parsley or fresh cilantro, finely chopped
- 2 cups water
- 2 garlic cloves, minced
- 2 tablespoons olive oil, divided
- 2 white onions, finely chopped
- 3 tablespoons green curry paste
- Salt and ground black pepper, to taste

Directions:

1. Sprinkle 1 tablespoon of olive oil in a deep cooking pan and warm on moderate heat.
2. Reduce the heat and cook the onions and garlic in the deep cooking pan using low heat for three to four minutes until translucent.
3. Then put the curry paste, coconut milk, parsley and water into the deep cooking pan. Bring them to a simmer for about three minutes.
4. Put in the chicken pieces and simmer for another six minutes until the chicken is thoroughly cooked.
5. In the meantime, warm the rest of the olive oil in a nonstick frying pan, then sauté the zucchini in the frying pan for about three minutes. Drizzle with salt and ground black pepper and sauté for another two minutes until tender.
6. Put in the cooked zucchini into the chicken broth and serve warm.

Nutritional Info: calories: 790 || total fat: 54g || net carbs: 18g || fiber: 5g || protein: 54g

Smoothies and Drinks

ALMOND BLUEBERRY SMOOTHIE

Time To Prepare: ten minutes

Time to Cook: 0 minutes

Yield: Servings 1

Ingredients:

- 1 banana
- 1 cup frozen blueberries
- 1 tbsp. almond butter
- 1/2 cup almond milk
- Water, as required

Directions:

1. Put in everything to a blender jug.
2. Cover the jug firmly.
3. Blend until the desired smoothness is achieved. Serve and enjoy!

Nutritional Info: Calories: 211 || Fat: 0.2 g || Protein: 5.6 g || Carbohydrates: 3.4 g || Fiber: 2.3 g

---

ALMOND BUTTER SMOOTHIES

Time To Prepare: five minutes

Time to Cook: 0 minutes

Yield: Servings 1

Ingredients:

- 1 banana, if possible frozen for a creamier shake
- 1 cup of hemp milk
- 1 scoop of hemp protein
- 1 Tablespoon natural almond butter
- few ice cubes

Directions:

Blend all ingredients together and enjoy!

Nutritional Info: Calories: 533 kcal **||** Protein: 31.23 g **||** Fat: 26.31 g **||** Carbohydrates: 47.13 g

---

APPLE CINNAMON WATER

Time To Prepare: five minutes

Time to Cook: five minutes

Yield: Servings 4

Ingredients:

- 1 whole apple, diced
- 5 cinnamon sticks
- Water to cover contents

Directions:

1. Put ingredients in the steamer basket. Put in pot.
2. Put in water cover contents.
3. Secure the lid. Cook on HIGH pressure five minutes.
4. When done, depressurize swiftly.
5. Remove steamer basket. Discard cooked produce.
6. Let flavored water cool. Chill completely before you serve.

Nutritional Info: Calories: 194 **||** Fat: 0g **||** Carbohydrates: 12g **||** Protein: 0g

---

BABY KALE PINEAPPLE SMOOTHIE

Time To Prepare: five minutes

Time to Cook: 0 minutes

Yield: Servings 1

Ingredients:

- 1 cup almond milk
- 1 cup Kale

- 1 tablespoon hemp protein powder
- 1/2 cup frozen pineapple

Directions:

Put the almond milk, pineapple, and greens in the blender and blend until the desired smoothness is achieved.

Nutritional Info: Calories: 389 kcal || Protein: 20.29 g || Fat: 16.2 g || Carbohydrates: 42.29 g

BEET AND CHERRY SMOOTHIE

Time To Prepare: five minutes

Time to Cook: 0 minutes

Yield: Servings 4

Ingredients:

- ½ cup frozen cherries, pitted
- ½ teaspoon frozen banana
- 1 tablespoon almond butter
- 10-ounce almond milk, unsweetened
- 2 small beets, peeled and slice into four

Directions:

1. Put in all ingredients in a blender.
2. Blend until the desired smoothness is achieved.

Nutritional Info: Calories 470 || Carbohydrates: 24 g || Fat: 38 g || Protein: 16 g

BEET SMOOTHIE

Time To Prepare: ten minutes

Time to Cook: 0 minutes

Yield: Servings 2

Ingredients:

- 1 tbsp. almond butter
- 1/2 banana, peeled and frozen
- 1/2 cup cherries, pitted
- 10 oz. almond milk, unsweetened
- 2 beets, peeled and quartered

Directions:

1. In your blender, combine the milk with the beets, banana, cherries, and butter.
2. Pulse thoroughly, pour into glasses, before you serve. Enjoy!

Nutritional Info: Calories: 165 || Fat: 5 g || Protein: 5 g || Carbohydrates: 22 g || Fiber: 6 g

---

BERRY SHRUB

Time To Prepare: ten minutes

Time to Cook: twenty minutes

Yield: Servings 4

Ingredients:

- ½ a cup of chopped fresh oregano
- 1 cup of dried elderberries
- 2 cups of apple cider vinegar
- 2 cups of honey
- 2 cups of water

Directions:

1. Put in listed ingredients to the instant pot.
2. Secure the lid. Cook on HIGH pressure twenty minutes.
3. When done, depressurize naturally.
4. Pour ingredients through a sieve into a jar.
5. Let cool down. Chill.

Nutritional Info: Calories: 127 || Fat: 0g || Carbohydrates: 6g || Protein: 0g

---

BLACKBERRY & GINGER MILKSHAKE

Time To Prepare: five minutes

Time to Cook: 0 minutes

Yield: Servings 2

Ingredients:

- 1 thumb-sized piece of ginger, grated
- 2 cups of almond milk
- 2 cups of blackberries, washed
- 2 cups of chopped peaches

Directions:

1. Combine all ingredients to a blender or juicer and blend until the desired smoothness is achieved.
2. Serve with a scattering of fresh blackberries and enjoy!

Nutritional Info: Calories: 619 kcal ‖ Protein: fifteen.42 g ‖ Fat: 11.63 g ‖ Carbohydrates: 123.04 g

---

BLACKBERRY ITALIAN DRINK

Time To Prepare: five minutes

Time to Cook: fifteen minutes

Yield: Servings 4

Ingredients:

- 1 bottle sparkling water
- 1 cup blackberries
- 1 lemon, cut
- 2 tbsp. honey

Directions:

1. Put in 1 cup (non-carbonated) water to the instant pot.
2. Put in blackberries to the instant pot.
3. Secure the lid. Cook on HIGH pressure ten minutes.

4. When done, depressurize naturally.
5. Mash the berries in the instant pot. Move to dish. Let cool.
6. As blackberries cook, in a separate small deep cooking pan with a heavy bottom. Put in honey. Simmer five minutes. Cool down.
7. To make the drink. Ladle 1 teaspoon honey. Pour in fruit mixture. Put in carbonated water. Stir.

Nutritional Info: Calories: 249 || Fat: 0.6g || Carbohydrates: 55g || Protein: 7.5g

BLENDED COCONUT MILK AND BANANA BREAKFAST SMOOTHIE

Time To Prepare: ten minutes

Time to Cook: 0 minutes

Yield: Servings 4

Ingredients:

- 2 cups almond milk
- 2 cups coconut milk
- 4 ripe moderate-sized bananas
- 4 tbsp. flax seeds
- 4 tsp. cinnamon

Directions:

1. Peel the banana and cut it into ½-inch pieces. Put all the ingredients in the blender and blend into a smoothie.
2. Put in a dash of cinnamon at the top of the smoothie before you serve.

Nutritional Info: Calories: 332 kcal || Protein: 12.49 g || Fat: 14.42 g || Carbohydrates: 42.46 g

BLUEBERRY AND SPINACH SHAKE

Time To Prepare: five minutes

Time to Cook: 0 minutes

Yield: Servings 2

Ingredients:

- 1 cup of low-fat Greek yogurt (not necessary)
- 1 cup of organic blueberries (or washed if non-organic)
- 1/2 cup of spinach
- ice cubes to the desired concentration

Directions:

1. Put in ingredients together in a blender until the desired smoothness is achieved and then serve in a tall glass.
2. Drizzle a few fresh berries on top if you prefer!

Nutritional Info: Calories: 233 kcal || Protein: 10.68 g || Fat: 5.38 g || Carbohydrates: 37.13 g

BLUEBERRY LIME JUICE

Time To Prepare: five minutes

Time to Cook: five minutes

Yield: Servings 4

Ingredients:

- 1 cup fresh blueberries
- Water to cover contents
- Zest and juice of 1 lime

Directions:

1. Put ingredients in a mesh steamer basket for instant pot. Put in pot.
2. Pour in water to immerse contents.
3. Secure the lid. Cook on HIGH pressure five minutes.
4. When done, depressurize swiftly.
5. Remove steamer basket. Discard cooked produce.
6. Let flavored water cool. Chill completely before you serve.

Nutritional Info: Calories: 86 || Fat: 0g || Carbohydrates: 22g || Protein: 0g

BLUEBERRY MATCHA SMOOTHIE

Time To Prepare: five minutes

Time to Cook: 0 minutes

Yield: Servings 2

Ingredients:

- ¼ Teaspoon Ground Cinnamon
- ¼ Teaspoon Ground Ginger
- 1 Banana
- 1 Tablespoon Chia Seeds
- 1 Tablespoon Matcha Powder
- 2 Cups Almond Milk
- 2 Cups Blueberries, Frozen
- 2 Tablespoons Protein Powder, Optional
- A Pinch Sea Salt

Directions:

Blend all ingredients until the desired smoothness is achieved.

Nutritional Info: Calories: 208 ‖ Protein: 8.7 Grams ‖ Fat: 5.7 Grams ‖ Carbohydrates: 31 Grams

---

BLUEBERRY POMEGRANATE SMOOTHIE

Time To Prepare: five minutes

Time to Cook: 0 minutes

Yield: Servings 2

Ingredients:

- ¼ cup of canned coconut milk
- 1 cup of pomegranate juice, unsweetened
- 1 tbsp. of hemp seeds
- 2 cup of frozen blueberries
- 6 to 8 ice cubes

Directions:

1. Mix the smoothie ingredients in your high-speed blender.
2. Pulse the ingredients a few times to cut them up.

3. Combine the mixture on the highest speed setting for thirty to 60 seconds.
4. Pour into glasses and serve.

Nutritional Info: Calories: 282 kcal **||** Protein: 5.64 g **||** Fat: 13.8 g **||** Carbohydrates: 37.75 g

---

BLUEBERRY SMOOTHIE

Time To Prepare: ten minutes

Time to Cook: 0 minutes

Yield: Servings 1

Ingredients:

- 1 banana, peeled
- 1 tbsp. almond butter
- 1 tsp. maca powder
- 1/2 cup almond milk, unsweetened
- 1/2 cup blueberries
- 1/2 cup water
- 1/4 tsp. ground cinnamon
- 2 handfuls baby spinach

Directions:

1. In your blender, combine the spinach with the banana, blueberries, almond butter, cinnamon, maca powder, water, and milk.
2. Pulse thoroughly, pour into a glass, before you serve. Enjoy!

Nutritional Info: Calories: 341 **||** Fat: 12 g **||** Protein: 10 g **||** Carbohydrates: 54 g **||** Fiber: 12 g

---

BROCCOLI SMOOTHIE

Time To Prepare: five minutes

Time to Cook: 0 minutes

Yield: Servings 4

Ingredients:

- 1 ½ cups strawberries
- 1 ½ cups water
- 1 cup broccoli florets
- 1 cup chopped spinach
- 2 bananas, cut, frozen
- 2 cups frozen mango chunks
- 2 cups pineapple juice

Directions:

1. Combine all ingredients into a blender and blend until the desired smoothness is achieved.
2. Pour into 4 tall glasses before you serve.

Nutritional Info: Calories: 222 kcal || Protein: 3.51 g || Fat: 1.98 g || Carbohydrates: 51.45 g

---

CARROT AND ORANGE TURMERIC DRINK

Time To Prepare: five minutes

Time to Cook: 0 minutes

Yield: Servings 2

Ingredients:

- 1 cup orange juice
- 1 tbsp. lemon juice
- 1/2 inch ginger slice
- 1/4 tsp. turmeric powder
- 2 carrots, peeled, chopped
- 2 tbsp. sugar

Directions:

1. In a blender, put in orange juice, sugar, turmeric powder, carrots, and lemon juice.
2. Blend well.

Serve!

Nutritional Info: Calories: 153 kcal || Protein: 4.47 g || Fat: 3.3 g || Carbohydrates: 27.02 g

CHERRY SMOOTHIE

Time To Prepare: five minutes

Time to Cook: 0 minutes

Yield: Servings 4-6

Ingredients:

- 1 ½ cups vanilla Greek yogurt
- 2 bananas, cut
- 3 cups cherry juice
- 3 cups pitted, froze dark sweet cherries
- Fresh cherries, pitted
- Mint sprigs
- To decorate: Optional

Directions:

1. Combine all ingredients into a blender and blend until the desired smoothness is achieved.
2. Pour into 4 tall glasses.
3. Decorate using optional ingredients if using before you serve.

Nutritional Info: Calories: 114 kcal || Protein: 2.36 g || Fat: 1.88 g || Carbohydrates: 23.49 g

CHOCOLATE CHERRY SMOOTHIE

Time To Prepare: five minutes

Time to Cook: 0 minutes

Yield: Servings 2

Ingredients:

- 2 cups almond milk, unsweetened
- 2 dates, pitted, chopped or 2 teaspoons pure maple syrup
- 2 scoops protein powder or 4 tablespoons almond butter (not necessary)
- 4 cups pitted, frozen cherries
- 4 tablespoons cocoa or cacao powder

- Cacao nibs
- Granola
- Hemp hearts
- To serve: Optional

Directions:

1. Combine all ingredients into a blender and blend until the desired smoothness is achieved.
2. Pour into 2 tall glasses and serve topped with optional ingredients.

Nutritional Info: Calories: 339 kcal **||** Protein: 16.37 g **||** Fat: 21.34 g **||** Carbohydrates: 27.99 g

---

CHOCOLATE LATTE WITH REISHI

Time To Prepare: five minutes

Time to Cook: ten minutes

Yield: Servings 2

Ingredients:

- 1 teaspoon Reishi powder
- 2 tablespoons coconut butter
- 4 cups almond milk, unsweetened
- 4 teaspoons raw cacao powder
- A pinch ground cinnamon
- A pinch sea salt
- Sweetener of your choice

Directions:

1. Put in almond milk into a deep cooking pan. Put the deep cooking pan using low heat.
2. When the milk is warm and just starts to bubble, remove the heat. Move into a blender.
3. Put in the remaining ingredients and blend for 30 – 40 seconds or until the desired smoothness is achieved.
4. Pour into mugs before you serve.

Nutritional Info: Calories: 461 kcal **||** Protein: 19.32 g **||** Fat: 30.57 g **||** Carbohydrates: 28.08 g

COOKED ICED TEA

Time To Prepare: two minutes

Time to Cook: 4 minutes

Yield: Servings 4

Ingredients:

- 2 tbsp. honey
- 4 regular tea bags
- 6 cups water

Directions:

1. Put in ingredients to the instant pot.
2. Secure the lid. Cook on HIGH pressure 4 minutes.
3. When done, depressurize naturally.
4. Allow to cool to room temperature. Serve over ice.

Nutritional Info: Calories: 22 || Fat: 0g || Carbohydrates: 6g || Protein: 0g

CUCUMBER KIWI GREEN SMOOTHIE

Time To Prepare: five minutes

Time to Cook: 0 minutes

Yield: Servings 2

Ingredients:

- ¼ cup of canned coconut milk
- 1 cup of coconut water
- 1 cup of seedless cucumber, chopped
- 2 ripe kiwi fruit
- 2 tbsps. of fresh chopped cilantro
- 6 to 8 ice cubes
- ice cubes

Directions:

1. Mix the smoothie ingredients in your high-speed blender.
2. Pulse the ingredients a few times to cut them up.
3. Combine the mixture on the highest speed setting for thirty to 60 seconds.
4. Pour into glasses and serve.

Nutritional Info: Calories: 140 kcal **||** Protein: 5.1 g **||** Fat: 10.52 g **||** Carbohydrates: 7.4 g

---

CUCUMBER MELON SMOOTHIE

Time To Prepare: five minutes

Time to Cook: 0 minutes

Yield: Servings 2

Ingredients:

- 1 ½ cups of chopped honeydew
- 1 cup of chilled coconut water
- 1 cup of seedless cucumber, diced
- 2 tbsp. of fresh mint
- 6 to 8 ice cubes

Directions:

1. Mix the smoothie ingredients in your high-speed blender.
2. Pulse the ingredients a few times to cut them up.
3. Combine the mixture on the highest speed setting for thirty to 60 seconds.
4. Pour into glasses and serve.

Nutritional Info: Calories: 300 kcal **||** Protein: 5.83 g **||** Fat: 8.55 g **||** Carbohydrates: 51.21 g

---

DREAMY YUMMY ORANGE CREAM SMOOTHIE

Time To Prepare: five minutes

Time to Cook: 0 minutes

Yield: Servings 2

Ingredients:

- ¼ cup of fresh orange juice
- ½ cup of canned full-fat coconut milk
- 1 cup of almond milk
- 1 navel orange, peel removed
- 6 to 8 ice cubes

Directions:

1. Mix the smoothie ingredients in your high-speed blender.
2. Pulse the ingredients a few times to cut them up.
3. Combine the mixture on the highest speed setting for thirty to 60 seconds.
4. Pour into glasses and serve.

Nutritional Info: Calories: 269 kcal **||** Protein: 8.63 g **||** Fat: 21.36 g **||** Carbohydrates: 12.75 g

---

FIG SMOOTHIE

Time To Prepare: five minutes

Time to Cook: 0 minutes

Yield: Servings 2

Ingredients:

- 1 Banana
- 1 Cup Almond Milk
- 1 Cup Whole Milk Yogurt, Plain
- 1 Tablespoon Almond Butter
- 1 Teaspoon Flaxseed, Ground
- 1 Teaspoon Honey, Raw
- 3-4 Ice Cubes
- 7 Figs, Halved (Fresh or Frozen)

Directions:

Blend all together ingredients until the desired smoothness is achieved, and serve instantly.

Nutritional Info: Calories: 362 **||** Protein: 9 Grams **||** Fat: 12 Grams **||** Carbohydrates: 60 Grams

FLU FIGHTING TONIC

Time To Prepare: five minutes

Time to Cook: ten minutes

Yield: Servings 2

Ingredients:

- ½ teaspoon turmeric powder
- 2 tablespoons clear honey if possible manuka
- Boiling water, as required
- Juice of 2 lemons
- Lemon slices to decorate

Directions:

1. Split the lemon juice into 2 mugs. Put in ¼ teaspoon turmeric powder into each mug.
2. Put in a tablespoon of honey into each mug.
3. Pour boiling water to fill up the mugs. Stir.
4. Decorate using a slice of lemon before you serve.

Nutritional Info: Calories: 123 kcal **||** Protein: 3.59 g **||** Fat: 3.23 g **||** Carbohydrates: 22.78 g

FRESH CRANBERRY AND LIME JUICE

Time To Prepare: five minutes

Time to Cook: 0 minutes

Yield: Servings 2

Ingredients:

- 1/2½ cups of mixed berries (frozen are fine)
- 1/2½ cups of spinach
- 2 limes, juiced
- 4 cups of cranberries

Directions:

Mix all the ingredients with water in a juicer until pureed and serve instantly over ice.

Nutritional Info: Calories: 578 kcal **||** Protein: 6.83 g **||** Fat: 9.92 g **||** Carbohydrates: 119.35 g

---

FRESH TROPICAL JUICE

Time To Prepare: five minutes

Time to Cook: 0 minutes

Yield: Servings 2

Ingredients:

- 1 whole pineapple, peeled and slice into chunks.
- 1 cup of water
- 1/2 can of low-fat coconut milk

Directions:

1. Put in all ingredients to a juicer and blend until the desired smoothness is achieved.
2. Serve over ice.

Nutritional Info: Calories: 116 kcal **||** Protein: 3.72 g **||** Fat: 3.13 g **||** Carbohydrates: 19.55 g

---

GINGER ALE

Time To Prepare: five minutes

Time to Cook: thirty minutes

Yield: Servings 4

Ingredients:

- 1 pound fresh ginger, unpeeled, diced
- 1 quart carbonated water
- 1 tbsp. honey
- Ice for serving
- Juice and rind of 2 lemons
- Lime wedges

Directions:

1. Put ginger and lemon juice in a food processor. Pulse to smooth consistency.

2. Move puree to the instant pot. Mix in honey.
3. Put in lemon peel to the instant pot.
4. Secure the lid. Cook on HIGH pressure thirty minutes.
5. When done, depressurize naturally. Strain and chill.
6. Serve over ice.

Nutritional Info: Calories: 108 || Fat: 0g || Carbohydrates: 28g || Protein: 0g

---

GINGER, CARROT, AND TURMERIC SMOOTHIE

Time To Prepare: five minutes

Time to Cook: 0 minutes

Yield: Servings 2

Ingredients:

- ½ cup Mango, fresh or frozen chunks
- 1 big Carrot, peeled and chopped
- 1 cup Coconut water
- 1 Orange, peeled and separated
- 1 tbsp. Hemp seeds, raw, shelled
- 1 tsp. Ginger, ground
- 1 tsp. Turmeric, ground
- 1/8 tsp. Cayenne pepper

Directions:

Puree all of the ingredients with one-half cup of ice until the desired smoothness is achieved and drink instantly.

Nutritional Info: Calories 250 || 35 grams sugar || 4.5 grams fat || 7 grams fiber || 48 grams carbs || 6 grams protein

---

GOLDEN CHAI LATTE

Time To Prepare: five minutes

Time to Cook: ten minutes

Yield: Servings 2

Ingredients:

- ¼ teaspoon ground cinnamon
- ½ cup water
- ½ tablespoon maple syrup
- ½ tablespoon turmeric powder
- 1 ¼ cups cashew milk or any other non-dairy milk of your choice
- 1 teaspoon loose leaf chai tea
- 1/8 teaspoon ground nutmeg
- A pinch ground cardamom

Directions:

1. Put in water and 1-cup milk into a deep cooking pan. Put the deep cooking pan on moderate heat.
2. Put in chai leaves in a tea strainer (the type that that has a lid and you can close). Lower the strainer in the deep cooking pan. Put in spices.
3. When it just comes to a light boil, remove the heat. Allow it to cool for five minutes. Take out the tea strainer and discard the leaves.
4. Put in maple syrup and stir.
5. Pour into glasses. Sprinkle remaining cashew milk on top. Decorate using cinnamon and nutmeg before you serve.

Nutritional Info: Calories: 142 kcal || Protein: 8.59 g || Fat: 6.26 g || Carbohydrates: 13.3 g

GREEN VANILLA SMOOTHIE

Time To Prepare: ten minutes

Time to Cook: 0 minutes

Yield: Servings 1

Ingredients:

- 1 1/2 cups fresh spinach leaves
- 1 banana, cut in chunks
- 1 cup grapes

- 1 tub (6 oz.) vanilla yogurt
- 1/2 apple, cored and chopped

Directions:

1. Put in everything to a blender jug.
2. Cover the jug firmly.
3. Blend until the desired smoothness is achieved. Serve and enjoy!

Nutritional Info: Calories: 131 || Fat: 0.2 g || Protein: 2.6 g || Carbohydrates: 9.1 g || Fiber: 1.3 g

---

HIBISCUS TEA

Time To Prepare: five minutes

Time to Cook: ten minutes

Yield: Servings 4

Ingredients:

- 1 tbsp. honey
- 1 tsp fresh ginger, grated
- 10 cups water
- 2 cup dried hibiscus petals
- Rind from 1 pineapple

Directions:

1. Wash hibiscus leaves meticulously with cold water.
2. Take away the dust.
3. Put in water, honey, and ginger to the instant pot. Stir.
4. Mix in hibiscus petals and pineapple rind.
5. Secure the lid. Cook on HIGH pressure ten minutes.
6. When done, depressurize naturally.
7. Remove pineapple rind. Pass liquid through a fine-mesh strainer.
8. Cool thoroughly. Chill before you serve.

Nutritional Info: Calories: 114 || Fat: 0g || Carbohydrates: 28g || Protein: 0g

HOT APPLE CIDER

Time To Prepare: five minutes

Time to Cook: fifteen minutes

Yield: Servings 4

Ingredients:

- ½ cup fresh cranberries
- ½ cup honey
- ½ star of anise
- ½ tsp whole cloves
- 1 lemon, peeled, cut into segments
- 1 orange, peeled, cut into segments
- 2 cinnamon sticks
- 7 medium apples, cored, quarter
- Water to cover ingredients

Directions:

1. Put in apples, lemon, orange, and cranberries to the instant pot.
2. Put in cinnamon stick, star anise, and cloves.
3. Pour in water to immerse ingredients.
4. Secure the lid. Cook on HIGH pressure fifteen minutes.
5. Depressurize naturally.
6. Mash fruit using a masher to release juices.
7. Strain the liquid. Chill completely before you serve.

Nutritional Info: Calories: 153 || Fat: 9g || Carbohydrates: 14g || Protein: 4g

HOT PEPPERMINT VANILLA LATTE

Time To Prepare: five minutes

Time to Cook: five minutes

Yield: Servings 4

Ingredients:

- ¼ cup honey
- 1 tsp vanilla
- 2 cups coffee
- 23 drops peppermint oil
- 4 cups almond milk

Directions:

1. Put in listed ingredients to the instant pot.
2. Secure the lid. Cook on HIGH pressure five minutes.
3. When done, depressurize naturally.
4. Serve warm.

Nutritional Info: Calories: 279 **||** Fat: 3g **||** Carbohydrates: 61g **||** Protein: 3g

---

INSTANT HORCHATA

Time To Prepare: five minutes

Time to Cook: five minutes

Yield: Servings 4

Ingredients:

- 1 cinnamon stick, broken into little chunks
- 32 ounces rice milk
- 6 tbsp. honey

Directions:

1. Put in listed ingredients to the instant pot.
2. Secure the lid. Cook on HIGH pressure five minutes.
3. When done, depressurize naturally over ten minutes.
4. Cool thoroughly. Chill before you serve.

Nutritional Info: Calories: 226 **||** Fat: 1g **||** Carbohydrates: 53g **||** Protein: 2g

---

JAMAICAN HIBISCUS TEA

Time To Prepare: five minutes

Time to Cook: five minutes

Yield: Servings 4

Ingredients:

- ½ tsp ginger, minced
- 1 cup dried hibiscus flowers
- 1 tbsp. honey
- 8 cups water
- Ice as required
- Juice of 1 lime

Directions:

1. Put in hibiscus flowers, water, honey, and ginger to the instant pot.
2. Secure the lid. Cook on HIGH pressure five minutes.
3. When done, depressurize naturally.
4. Cool thoroughly. Move to glass decanter. Mix in lime Juice. Pour over ice.

Nutritional Info: Calories: 197 || Fat: 0g || Carbohydrates: 18g || Protein: 0g

---

KALE SMOOTHIE

Time To Prepare: ten minutes

Time to Cook: 0 minutes

Yield: Servings 2

Ingredients:

- 10 kale leaves
- 2 pears, chopped
- 5 bananas, peeled and slice into chunks
- 5 cups almond milk
- 5 tbsp. almond butter

Directions:

1. In your blender, combine the kale with the bananas, pears, almond butter, and almond milk.

2. Pulse thoroughly, split into glasses, before you serve. Enjoy!

Nutritional Info: Calories: 267 || Fat: 11 g || Protein: 7 g || Carbohydrates: fifteen g || Fiber: 7 g

---

KIWI STRAWBERRY SMOOTHIE

Time To Prepare: ten minutes

Time to Cook: 0 minutes

Yield: Servings 1

Ingredients:

- ¼ cup Chia seed powder
- ½ cup Strawberries, fresh or frozen, chopped
- 1 Banana, diced
- 1 cup Milk, almond or coconut
- 1 Kiwi, peeled and chopped
- 1 tsp. Basil, ground
- 1 tsp. Turmeric, ground

Directions:

Drink instantly after all the ingredients have been thoroughly combined.

Nutritional Info: Calories 250 || 9.9 grams sugar || 1 gram fat || 34 grams carbs || 4.3 grams fiber ||

LEMON GINGER ICED TEA

Time To Prepare: five minutes

Time to Cook: ten minutes

Yield: Servings 2-3

Ingredients:

- ¼ teaspoon turmeric
- 1 tablespoon fresh lemon juice or to taste (not necessary)
- 1 tablespoon maple syrup

- 2 – 3 lemon slices
- 2 inches fresh ginger, peeled, thinly cut or to taste
- 3-4 cups water
- A pinch ground cinnamon

Directions:

1. Pour water into a deep cooking pan. Put in ginger, turmeric, lemon slices, and cinnamon. Put the deep cooking pan on moderate heat.
2. Cover and simmer for eight - ten minutes.
3. Strain and pour into a jar. Place the maple syrup, and lemon juice, then stir. Chill for eight – 10 hours.
4. Stir thoroughly. Pour into glasses before you serve.

Nutritional Info: Calories: 55 kcal || Protein: 2.32 g || Fat: 2.13 g || Carbohydrates: 7.47 g

---

MANGO AND GINGER INFUSED WATER

Time To Prepare: five minutes

Time to Cook: five minutes

Yield: Servings 4

Ingredients:

- 1 cup fresh mango, chopped
- 2-inch piece ginger, peeled, cubed
- Water to cover ingredients

Directions:

1. Put ingredients in the mesh steamer basket.
2. Put basket in the instant pot.
3. Put in water to immerse contents.
4. Secure the lid. Cook on HIGH pressure five minutes.
5. When done, depressurize swiftly.
6. Remove steamer basket. Discard cooked produce.
7. Let flavored water cool. Chill completely and serve.

Nutritional Info: Calories: 209 **||** Fat: 1g **||** Carbohydrates: 51g **||** Protein: 2g

---

MANGO TOMATO SMOOTHIE

Time To Prepare: five minutes

Time to Cook: 0 minutes

Yield: Servings 4

Ingredients:

- 1 cup almond milk
- 2 cups chopped cilantro
- 2 cups pineapple chunks
- 2 mangoes, peeled, pitted
- 4 Campari tomatoes, chopped
- 6 cups fresh baby spinach

Directions:

1. Combine all ingredients into a blender and blend until the desired smoothness is achieved.
2. Pour into 4 tall glasses before you serve.

Nutritional Info: Calories: 395 kcal **||** Protein: 13.1 g **||** Fat: 8.19 g **||** Carbohydrates: 73.65 g

---

MIXED FRUIT & NUT MILKSHAKE

Time To Prepare: five minutes

Time to Cook: 0 minutes

Yield: Servings 2

Ingredients:

- 1 tbsp. of honey
- 1/2 cup of almond milk
- 1½ grapefruit; peeled and chopped
- 1/2½ inch piece of ginger, minced

- 12 strawberries
- 2 tbsp. of chopped almonds
- juice of 1 orange

Directions:

1. Put everything but the strawberries in a blender until the desired smoothness is achieved.
2. Put in in the strawberries and blend until pureed, serving in a tall glass.

Nutritional Info: Calories: 140 kcal **||** Protein: 5.89 g **||** Fat: 5.84 g **||** Carbohydrates: 17.36 g

PARSLEY GINGER GREEN JUICE

Time To Prepare: five minutes

Time to Cook: 0 minutes

Yield: Servings 2

Ingredients:

- 2 cucumbers, chopped
- 2 green apples, cored
- 2 lemons, peeled, halved
- 4 cups chopped parsley
- 4 cups chopped spinach
- 4 inches fresh ginger, peeled, cut
- 6 stalks celery, chopped

Directions:

1. Juice together all the ingredients in a juicer.
2. Pour into 2 glasses before you serve.

Nutritional Info: Calories: 239 kcal **||** Protein: 10.74 g **||** Fat: 5.08 g **||** Carbohydrates: 44.86 g

PEACH AND RASPBERRY LEMONADE

Time To Prepare: five minutes

Time to Cook: five minutes

Yield: Servings 4

Ingredients:

- ½ cup fresh raspberries
- 1 cup fresh peaches, chopped
- Water to cover ingredients
- Zest and juice of 1 lemon

Directions:

1. Put ingredients in mesh basket for instant pot. Put in pot.
2. Put in water to barely cover the fruit.
3. Secure the lid. Cook on HIGH pressure five minutes.
4. When done, depressurize swiftly.
5. Remove steamer basket. Discard cooked produce.
6. Let flavored water cool. Chill completely before you serve.

Nutritional Info: Calories: 77 || Fat: 0g || Carbohydrates: 19g || Protein: 0g

---

PEACH MAPLE SMOOTHIE

Time To Prepare: ten minutes

Time to Cook: 0 minutes

Yield: Servings 1

Ingredients:

- 1 cup fat-free yogurt
- 1 cup ice
- 2 tbsp. maple syrup
- 4 big peaches, peeled and chopped

Directions:

1. Put in everything to a blender jug.
2. Cover the jug firmly.
3. Blend until the desired smoothness is achieved. Serve and enjoy!

Nutritional Info: Calories: 125 || Fat: 0.4 g || Protein: 5.6 g || Carbohydrates: 8 g || Fiber: 2.3 g

---

PEACHY KEEN SMOOTHIE

Time To Prepare: five minutes

Time to Cook: 0 minutes

Yield: Servings 2

Ingredients:

- 1 ½ cups of frozen peaches
- 1 cup of almond milk
- 1 small frozen banana
- 2 tbsp. of raw hemp seeds
- 6 to 8 ice cubes
- Pinch of ground ginger

Directions:

1. Mix the smoothie ingredients in your high-speed blender.
2. Pulse the ingredients a few times to cut them up.
3. Combine the mixture on the highest speed setting for thirty to 60 seconds.
4. Pour into glasses and serve.

Nutritional Info: Calories: 388 kcal || Protein: 10.59 g || Fat: 11.93 g || Carbohydrates: 64.08 g

---

PINEAPPLE & GINGER JUICE

Time To Prepare: five minutes

Time to Cook: 0 minutes

Yield: Servings 2

Ingredients:

- 2 apples, cored, chopped
- 2 cucumbers, chopped
- 2 cups chopped pineapple

- 2 cups spinach
- 2 inches ginger, peeled, cut
- 2 lemons, peeled, halved
- 8 celery stalks, chopped

Directions:

1. Juice together all the ingredients in a juicer.
2. Pour into 2 glasses before you serve.

Nutritional Info: Calories: 339 kcal **||** Protein: 7.44 g **||** Fat: 4.23 g **||** Carbohydrates: 75.38 g

PINEAPPLE AND GREENS SMOOTHIE

Time To Prepare: five minutes

Time to Cook: 0 minutes

Yield: Servings 2

Ingredients:

- ¾ cup of almond milk
- 1 cup of chopped spinach
- 1 cup of frozen pineapple
- 1 small frozen banana
- 1 tbsp. of honey
- 2 tbsp. Of chia seeds

Directions:

1. Mix the smoothie ingredients in your high-speed blender.
2. Pulse the ingredients a few times to cut them up.
3. Combine the mixture on the highest speed setting for thirty to 60 seconds.
4. Pour into glasses and serve.

Nutritional Info: Calories: 272 kcal **||** Protein: 5.27 g **||** Fat: 4.5 g **||** Carbohydrates: 56.37 g

PINEAPPLE- GINGER SMOOTHIE

Time To Prepare: five minutes

Time to Cook: 0 minutes

Yield: Servings 1

Ingredients:

- ½ inch thick ginger, cut
- 1 cup coconut milk
- 1 cup pineapple slice

Directions:

1. Put all ingredients in a blender.
2. Pulse until the desired smoothness is achieved.
3. Chill before you serve.

Nutritional Info: Calories 299 || Fat: 8 g || Protein: 9 g || Carbohydrates: 51 g

---

PINEAPPLE SMOOTHIE

Time To Prepare: ten minutes

Time to Cook: 0 minutes

Yield: Servings 2

Ingredients:

- 1 1/2 cups pineapple chunks
- 1 cup coconut water
- 1 orange, peeled and slice into quarters
- 1 tbsp. fresh grated ginger
- 1 tsp. chia seeds
- 1 tsp. turmeric powder
- A pinch black pepper

Directions:

1. In your blender, combine the coconut water with the orange, pineapple, ginger, chia seeds, turmeric, and black pepper.
2. Pulse thoroughly, pour into a glass.

Makes for a great breakfast!

Nutritional Info: Calories: 151 || Fat: 2 g || Protein: 4 g || Carbohydrates: 12 g || Fiber: 6 g

---

PINK CALIFORNIA SMOOTHIE

Time To Prepare: ten minutes

Time to Cook: 0 minutes

Yield: Servings 1

Ingredients:

- 1 container (8 oz.) lemon yogurt
- 1/3 cup orange juice
- 7 big strawberries

Directions:

1. Put in everything to a blender jug.
2. Cover the jug firmly.
3. Blend until the desired smoothness is achieved. Serve and enjoy!

Nutritional Info: Calories: 144 || Fat: 0.4 g || Protein: 5.6 g || Carbohydrates: 8 g || Fiber: 2.3 g

---

PUMPKIN PIE SMOOTHIE

Time To Prepare: five minutes

Time to Cook: 0 minutes

Yield: Servings 2

Ingredients:

- ½ Cup Pumpkin, Canned & Unsweetened
- 1 Banana
- 1 Cup Almond Milk
- 1 Teaspoon Ground Cinnamon
- 1 Teaspoon Ground Nutmeg
- 1 Teaspoon Maple Syrup, Pure

- 1 Teaspoon Vanilla Extract Pure
- 2 Tablespoons Almond Butter, Heaping
- 2-3 Ice Cubes

Directions:

Blend all ingredients together until the desired smoothness is achieved.

Nutritional Info: Calories: 235 || Protein: 5.6 Grams || Fat: 11 Grams || Carbohydrates: 27.8 Grams

---

PURPLE FRUIT SMOOTHIE

Time To Prepare: ten minutes

Time to Cook: 0 minutes

Yield: Servings 1

Ingredients:

- 2 frozen bananas, cut in chunks
- 1 cup orange juice
- 1 tbsp. honey, optional
- 1 tsp. vanilla extract, optional
- 1/2 cup frozen blueberries

Directions:

1. Put in everything to a blender jug.
2. Cover the jug firmly.
3. Blend until the desired smoothness is achieved. Serve and enjoy!

Nutritional Info: Calories: 133 || Fat: 1.1 g || Protein: 3.6 g || Carbohydrates: 7.6 g || Fiber: 1.3 g

---

RASPBERRY BANANA SMOOTHIE

Time To Prepare: ten minutes

Time to Cook: 0 minutes

Yield: Servings 1

Ingredients:

- 1 banana
- 1 cup almond milk
- 1 cup frozen raspberries
- 1 cup raspberry yogurt
- 1 tbsp. flaxseed meal
- 1/4 cup Concord grape juice
- 1/4 cup rolled oats
- 16 whole almonds

Directions:

1. Put in everything to a blender jug.
2. Cover the jug firmly.
3. Blend until the desired smoothness is achieved and then serve. Enjoy!

Nutritional Info: Calories: 214 || Fat: 0.4 g || Protein: 5.6 g || Carbohydrates: 8 g || Fiber: 2.3 g

---

RASPBERRY SMOOTHIE

Time To Prepare: ten minutes

Time to Cook: 0 minutes

Yield: Servings 2

Ingredients:

- 1 avocado, pitted and peeled
- 1/2 cup raspberries
- 3/4 cup raspberry juice
- 3/4 cup orange juice

Directions:

1. In your blender, combine the avocado with the raspberry juice, orange juice, and raspberries.
2. Pulse thoroughly, split into 2 glasses, before you serve. Enjoy!

Nutritional Info: Calories: 125 || Fat: 11 g || Protein: 3 g || Carbohydrates: 9 g || Fiber: 7 g

SPICY TOMATO SMOOTHIE

Time To Prepare: five minutes

Time to Cook: 0 minutes

Yield: Servings 2

Ingredients:

- ¼ cup chopped red onion
- 1 jalapeño, cut, deseed if you wish
- 1 small bunch cilantro, chopped
- 1 small cucumber
- 2 big carrots, chopped
- 2 cloves garlic, peeled
- 6 small vine tomatoes
- Juice of 2 limes

Directions:

1. Combine all ingredients into a blender and blend until the desired smoothness is achieved.
2. Pour into 2 tall glasses before you serve.

Nutritional Info: Calories: 269 kcal || Protein: 24.87 g || Fat: 8.71 g || Carbohydrates: 26.89 g

STRAWBERRY OATMEAL SMOOTHIE

Time To Prepare: ten minutes

Time to Cook: 0 minutes

Yield: Servings 1

Ingredients:

- 1 cup soy milk
- 1 banana, broken into chunks
- 14 frozen strawberries
- 1/2 cup rolled oats
- 1/2 tsp. vanilla extract

- 1 1/2 tsp. honey

Directions:

1. Put in everything to a blender jug.
2. Cover the jug firmly.
3. Blend until the desired smoothness is achieved. Serve and enjoy!

Nutritional Info: Calories: 172 || Fat: 0.4 g || Protein: 5.6 g || Carbohydrates: 8 g || Fiber: 2 g

---

SWEET & SAVOURY SMOOTHIE

Time To Prepare: five minutes

Time to Cook: 0 minutes

Yield: Servings 2

Ingredients:

- 1 apple, peeled and cut
- 1 banana, peeled and cut
- 1 cup of almond or soy milk
- 1 cup of fresh pineapple, peeled and cut
- 1 tbsp. of lemon juice
- 1/2 tbsp. of ginger, grated
- 1/4 tsp of ground turmeric
- 2 cups of carrots, peeled and cut
- 2 cups of filtered water.

Directions:

1. Blend carrots and water to make a pureed carrot juice.
2. Pour into a Mason jar or sealable container, cover, and store in the refrigerator.
3. When done, put in the rest of the smoothie ingredients to a blender or juicer until the desired smoothness is achieved.
4. Put in the carrot juice in at the end, blending meticulously until the desired smoothness is achieved.
5. Serve with or without ice.

Nutritional Info: Calories: 225 kcal **||** Protein: 6.03 g **||** Fat: 5.78 g **||** Carbohydrates: 39.93 g

---

SWEET CRANBERRY JUICE

Time To Prepare: five minutes

Time to Cook: 8 minutes

Yield: Servings 4

Ingredients:

- ½ cup honey
- 1 cinnamon stick
- 1 gallon filtered water
- 4 cups fresh cranberries
- Juice of 1 lemon

Directions:

1. Put in cranberries, ½ of water, cinnamon cling to the instant pot.
2. Secure the lid. Cook on HIGH pressure 8 minutes.
3. Depressurize naturally.
4. Once cool, strain liquid. Put in remaining water.
5. Mix in honey and lemon. Cool thoroughly.
6. Chill before you serve.

Nutritional Info: Calories: 184 **||** Fat: 0g **||** Carbohydrates: 49g **||** Protein: 1g

---

TRIPLE FRUIT SMOOTHIE

Time To Prepare: ten minutes

Time to Cook: 0 minutes

Yield: Servings 1

Ingredients:

- 1 banana, peeled and chopped
- 1 container (8 oz.) peach yogurt
- 1 cup ice cubes

- 1 cup strawberries
- 1 kiwi, cut
- 1/2 cup blueberries
- 1/2 cup orange juice

Directions:

1. Put in everything to a blender jug.
2. Cover the jug firmly.
3. Blend until the desired smoothness is achieved. Serve and enjoy!

Nutritional Info: Calories: 124 || Fat: 0.4 g || Protein: 5.6 g || Carbohydrates: 8 g || Fiber: 2.3 g

---

TROPICAL MANGO COCONUT SMOOTHIE

Time To Prepare: five minutes

Time to Cook: 0 minutes

Yield: Servings 2

Ingredients:

- ½ cup of canned coconut milk
- ½ cup of fresh orange juice
- 1 ½ cups of frozen mango
- 1 ½ tsp of honey
- 1 medium frozen banana
- 1 tbsp. of fresh lemon juice

Directions:

1. Mix the smoothie ingredients in your high-speed blender.
2. Pulse the ingredients a few times to cut them up.
3. Combine the mixture on the highest speed setting for thirty to 60 seconds.
4. Pour into glasses and serve.

Nutritional Info: Calories: 354 kcal || Protein: 6.7 g || Fat: 18.09 g || Carbohydrates: 47.42 g

---

TROPICAL PINEAPPLE KIWI SMOOTHIE

Time To Prepare: five minutes

Time to Cook: 0 minutes

Yield: Servings 2

Ingredients:

- 1 ½ cup of frozen pineapple
- 1 cup of canned full-fat coconut milk
- 1 ripe kiwi; peeled and chopped
- 1 tsp of spirulina powder
- 3 tsp of lime juice
- 6 to 8 ice cubes

Directions:

1. Mix the smoothie ingredients in your high-speed blender.
2. Pulse the ingredients a few times to cut them up.
3. Combine the mixture on the highest speed setting.
4. Pour into glasses and serve.

Nutritional Info: Calories: 480 kcal || Protein: 7.38 g || Fat: 31.92 g || Carbohydrates: 48.35 g

---

TURMERIC AND GINGER TONIC

Time To Prepare: five minutes

Time to Cook: ten minutes

Yield: Servings 4

Ingredients:

- 1/8 teaspoon cayenne pepper
- 2 tablespoons grated, fresh ginger
- 2 tablespoons grated, fresh turmeric
- 6 cups water
- Juice of 2 lemons
- Maple syrup or honey to taste
- The rind of 2 lemons, peeled

Directions:

1. Put in water, ginger, turmeric, cayenne pepper, and lemon rind into a deep cooking pan.
2. Put the deep cooking pan on moderate to high heat. (Do not boil)
3. Once the mixture is hot, remove from heat.
4. Strain into 4 mugs. Put in honey and lemon juice and stir.
5. Serve warm.

Nutritional Info: Calories: 48 kcal **||** Protein: 2.28 g **||** Fat: 1.81 g **||** Carbohydrates: 7.03 g

---

TURMERIC DELIGHT

Time To Prepare: five minutes

Time to Cook: 0 minutes

Yield: Servings 2

Ingredients:

- ¼ Teaspoon Ginger
- ½ Teaspoon Cinnamon
- 1 Banana, Sliced
- 1 Tablespoon Lemon Juice, Fresh
- 1 Teaspoon Turmeric
- 2 Cups Yogurt, Plain & Whole Milk
- 2 Teaspoons Honey, Raw

Directions:

Combine all ingredients into a blender then blend until the desired smoothness is achieved.

Nutritional Info: Calories: 234 **||** Protein: 9.3 Grams **||** Fat: 8.2 Grams **||** Carbohydrates: 33.5 Grams

---

TURMERIC HOT CHOCOLATE

Time To Prepare: five minutes

Time to Cook: ten minutes

Yield: Servings 2

Ingredients:

- 1/8 tsp. cayenne pepper, optional
- 1/8 tsp. pepper
- 2 cups milk
- 2 tsp. ground turmeric
- 3 tbsp. cacao or cocoa powder
- 4 tsp. coconut oil
- 4 tsp. honey

Directions:

1. Put in milk, turmeric, cocoa, and coconut oil into a deep cooking pan. Put the deep cooking pan on moderate heat. Coconut oil and pepper are added because it helps to absorb the turmeric.
2. Whisk regularly until well blended.
3. When it starts to boil, remove from heat. Put in honey, cayenne pepper, and pepper and whisk well.
4. Split into 2 cups before you serve.

Nutritional Info: Calories: 339 kcal **||** Protein: 12.76 g **||** Fat: 21.19 g **||** Carbohydrates: 30.35 g

---

TURMERIC TEA

Time To Prepare: five minutes

Time to Cook: fifteen minutes

Yield: Servings 2

Ingredients:

- ½ teaspoon ground ginger
- ½ teaspoon turmeric powder
- ½ tsp ground cinnamon
- 2 cups water
- 2 lemon juices
- 2 tablespoons honey

Directions:

1. Put in water into a deep cooking pan. Put the deep cooking pan on moderate heat.
2. When it starts to boil, put in turmeric, cinnamon, and ginger and stir slowly.
3. Remove the heat. Cover and allow the mixture to steep for 12 – fifteen minutes. Put in honey and lemon juice.
4. Stir and pour into mugs.
5. Serve.

Nutritional Info: Calories: 121 kcal ‖ Protein: 3.57 g ‖ Fat: 3.2 g ‖ Carbohydrates: 21.97 g

VANILLA AVOCADO SMOOTHIE

Time To Prepare: ten minutes

Time to Cook: 0 minutes

Yield: Servings 1

Ingredients:

- 1 cup almond milk
- 1 ripe avocado, halved and pitted
- 1/2 cup vanilla yogurt
- 3 tbsp. honey
- 8 ice cubes

Directions:

1. Put in everything to a blender jug.
2. Cover the jug firmly.
3. Blend until the desired smoothness is achieved. Serve and enjoy!

Nutritional Info: Calories: 143 ‖ Fat: 1.2 g ‖ Protein: 4.6 g ‖ Carbohydrates: 21 g ‖ Fiber: 2.3 g

VANILLA BLUEBERRY SMOOTHIE

Time To Prepare: five minutes

Time to Cook: 0 minutes

Yield: Servings 1

Ingredients:

- 1 cup fresh blueberries
- 1 tbsp. flaxseed oil
- 2 cups hemp milk
- 2 tbsp. hemp protein powder
- Handful of ice/ 1 cup frozen blueberries

Directions:

1. Mix milk and fresh blueberries plus ice (or frozen blueberries) in a blender.
2. Blend for a minute, move to a glass, and mix in flaxseed oil.

Nutritional Info: Calories: 1041 kcal ‖ Protein: 35.21 g ‖ Fat: 41.04 g ‖ Carbohydrates: 140.4 g

VANILLA TURMERIC ORANGE JUICE

Time To Prepare: five minutes

Time to Cook: 0 minutes

Yield: Servings 2

Ingredients:

- ½ teaspoon turmeric powder
- 1 teaspoon ground cinnamon
- 2 cups unsweetened almond milk
- 2 teaspoons vanilla extract
- 6 oranges, peeled, separated into segments, deseeded
- Pepper to taste

Directions:

1. Juice the oranges. Put in the remaining ingredients.
2. Pour into 2 glasses before you serve.

Nutritional Info: Calories: 223 kcal ‖ Protein: 11.47 g ‖ Fat: 11.79 g ‖ Carbohydrates: fifteen.9 g

VOLUPTUOUS VANILLA HOT DRINK

Time To Prepare: ten minutes

Time to Cook: 0 minutes

Yield: Servings 1

Ingredients:

- 1 scoop of hemp protein
- 1/2 Tbsp. ground cinnamon (or more to taste)
- 1/2 Tbsp. vanilla extract
- 3 cups unsweetened almond milk (or 1 1/2 cup full-fat coconut milk + 1 1/2 cups water)
- Stevia to taste

Directions:

1. Put the almond milk into a pitcher. Put ground cinnamon, hemp, vanilla extract in a small deep cooking pan on moderate to high heat. Heat until the pure liquid stevia is just melted and then pour the pure liquid stevia mixture into the pitcher.
2. Stir until the pure liquid stevia is well blended with the almond milk. Bring the pitcher in your refrigerator and let it cool for minimum two hours. Stir thoroughly before you serve.

Nutritional Info: Calories: 656 kcal || Protein: 42.12 g || Fat: 33.05 g || Carbohydrates: 44.45 g

---

WASSAIL

Time To Prepare: five minutes

Time to Cook: ten minutes

Yield: Servings 4

Ingredients:

- ½ tsp nutmeg
- 1 inch peeled ginger
- 10 cloves
- 2 vanilla beans, split or 2 Tbsp pure vanilla extract
- 4 cups orange juice
- 5 cinnamon sticks
- 8 cups apple cider

- Zest and juice of 2 lemons

Directions:

1. Pour cider and orange juice in the instant pot.
2. Put cinnamon sticks, nutmeg piece, cloves, lemon zest, vanilla beans in the steamer basket.
3. If you didn't use vanilla beans, pour in vanilla extract. Put in lemon juice.
4. Secure the lid. Cook on HIGH pressure ten minutes.
5. When done, depressurize naturally.
6. Discard contents of the steamer basket.
7. Serve hot from the pot.

Nutritional Info: Calories: 221 || Fat: 0g || Carbohydrates: 42g || Protein: 0g

---

WHITE HOT CHOCOLATE

Time To Prepare: five minutes

Time to Cook: six minutes

Yield: Servings 2

Ingredients:

- ¼ cup cocoa powder/butter
- 2 - 2½ Tbsp honey
- 2 tsp vanilla extract
- 3 cups coconut milk
- Pinch of sea salt

Directions:

1. Put in milk, cocoa powder/butter, honey, vanilla extract, and salt to the instant pot.
2. Secure the lid. Cook on LOW pressure six minutes.
3. Depressurize swiftly.
4. Use a hand blender to blend contents 25 seconds.
5. Serve hot.

Nutritional Info: Calories: 331 || Fat: 14g || Carbohydrates: 47g || Protein: 4g

WONDERFUL WATERMELON DRINK

Time To Prepare: five minutes

Time to Cook: 0 minutes

Yield: Servings 2

Ingredients:

- 1 cup of coconut water
- 1 cup of watermelon chunks
- 1/2 cup of tart cherries
- 2 cups of frozen mixed berries
- 2 tbsp. of chia seeds

Directions:

1. Combine all ingredients in a blender or juicer then blend until pureed.
2. Serve instantly and enjoy!

Nutritional Info: Calories: 330 kcal || Protein: 10.22 g || Fat: 9.71 g || Carbohydrates: 53.3 g

ZESTY CITRUS SMOOTHIE

Time To Prepare: five minutes

Time to Cook: 0 minutes

Yield: Servings 1

Ingredients:

- 1 cup almond milk
- 1 med orange peeled, cleaned, and cut into sections
- 1 tbsp. flaxseed oil
- 2 tsp hemp protein powder
- half cup lemon juice
- Handful of ice

Directions:

1. Mix milk, lemon juice, orange, and ice in a blender.

2. Blend for a minute, move to a glass, and mix in flaxseed oil.

Nutritional Info: Calories: 427 kcal **||** Protein: 17.5 g **||** Fat: 28.88 g **||** Carbohydrates: 24.96 g

ABOUT THE AUTHOR

Stephanie Bennett is an American health coach, foodie, and author based in New York. She enjoys sharing simple, delicious recipes with her readers, and coming up with new ways to help people live a healthier life.